Change Management *A*

Leadership of Change® Volume 5

by

Peter F. Gallagher

Change Management Adoption: For change adoption to be successful, the leaders, sponsor and change team should support employees through the change transition by providing **A**wareness, **U**nderstanding, **I**nvolvement, **L**earning, and **M**otivation using the AUILM® Employee Change Adoption Model.

Change Management Body of Knowledge (CMBoK) Volume 5

PFG Publishing

Enabling the Leadership of Change®

Change Waits for No Leader

Leadership of Change®

Change Management Body of Knowledge (CMBoK)

If more employees were better leaders of change, the organisational benefits would be endless. We enable the Leadership of Change®

The **Leadership of Change®** encompasses practical change management concepts, models, depictions, assessments, tools, templates, checklists, plans, a roadmap and glossary structured around the ten-step **a2B Change Management Framework®** (**a2BCMF®**). The delivery vehicles are change management books, change management gamification manuals, change management gamification workshops (face-to-face/virtual), leadership alignment workshops and masterclasses.

The **Leadership of Change®** is both thought leadership and a suite of tools to propel you from where your organisation is right now, the current 'a' state, to where you want to be, the future 'B' state. The **Leadership of Change®** will help you to implement your organisation's change or improvement and achieve a 100% return on investment (ROI) with full employee adoption, enabling you to secure future profit and remain ahead of your competitors. Truly great **Leadership of Change®** combines thoughtful strategy alignment of your leadership team and change leadership skills to lead employee change adoption and employee behaviour change.

Leadership of Change® Volumes: The **Change Management Body of Knowledge** (**CMBoK**) volumes are intended to be leading practice in organisational change management and implementation, which support strategy execution. They are based on the author's work, with over thirty years of organisational change implementation, transformation, and business improvement experience in over thirty countries.

Volumes 1 - 7 focus on learning about the practical implementation of change management. The books cover Change Management: Fables, Pocket Guide, Handbook, Leadership, Adoption, Behaviour and Sponsorship.

Volumes A - E are workshop manuals that focus on using change management gamification to learn about change leadership, employee change adoption and employee behaviour change.

Change Management Adoption

Leadership of Change® Volume 5
Change Management Body of Knowledge (CMBoK) Volume 5

Change Management Adoption: Achieving employee change adoption in a major organisation change or transformation has mixed success, and the return on investment (ROI) benefits are not always realised. For change adoption to be successful, the leaders, sponsor and change team should support employees through the change transition by providing **A**wareness, **U**nderstanding, **I**nvolvement, **L**earning, and **M**otivation using the **AUILM®** Employee Change Adoption Model.

About this Book

Organisations are operating in an environment of rapid change and transformation, where success is dependent on employees adopting the new technology or way of working to improve operating performance and achieve the targeted ROI. The fact that successful implementation of the change or transformation is critical to the future viability of the organisation is sometimes not enough.

The **Leadership of Change® Volume 5** focuses on how to achieve employee change adoption in a major organisation change or transformation using the **AUILM® Employee Change Adoption Model**. The **AUILM® Model** outlines the five key life cycle steps the employee goes through in the change transition. The model helps change teams to understand how employees tend to react during change and then supports them through the change, so resistance is minimised, and adoption is maximised. For change adoption to be successful, employees should be supported through the change transition, being provided with **A**wareness, **U**nderstanding, **I**nvolvement, **L**earning, and **M**otivation so the organisation can achieve sustainable change and benefits realisation. Change implementation focuses on aligning employees, processes, systems and leaders, it is also supported by the **a2B Change Management Framework®** (a2BCMF®).

Copyright ©

Change Management Adoption - Leadership of Change® Volume 5

All rights reserved. No part of this work may be used or reproduced by any means: graphic, electronic, or mechanical, including photocopying, recording, taping, or by any information storage retrieval system without the written permission of the publisher except in the case of brief quotations embodied in critical articles and reviews.

www.peterfgallagher.com/leadership-of-change

and

www.a2B.consulting

The following are registered trademarks:
a2B Change Management Framework® (a2BCMF®)
AMI® Change Management Leadership Model
a2B3S® Change Management Sponsorship Model
a2B5R® Behaviour Change Model
AUILM® Change Adoption Model

This book was created and written by Peter F Gallagher.

This book is suitable for leaders of change, organisational leadership teams, business professionals undertaking organisational change management, transformation, and improvement, or for students studying change management. It is typically sold or distributed under, or as part of, a licence agreement to learn how to use the models, frameworks, methods, and practices contained herein.

Copyright © 2021 Peter F Gallagher and a2B.consulting
All rights reserved
ISBN-13: 9798554912610
Publisher: PFG Publishing

Disclaimer

Descriptions and other related information in this document are provided only to illustrate the methods covered. You are fully responsible for the use of these methods. peterfgallagher.com and a2B.consulting assumes no responsibility for any losses incurred by you or any third parties arising from the use of these methods or information.

We have used reasonable care in preparing the information included in this book, but peterfgallagher.com and a2B.consulting does not warrant that such information is error free. We assume no liability whatsoever for any damages incurred by you resulting from errors in, or omissions from the information included herein.

peterfgallagher.com and a2B.consulting does not assume any liability for the infringement of patents, copyrights, or other intellectual property rights of third parties by or arising from the use of peterfgallagher.com and a2B.consulting information described in this document. No license, express, implied or otherwise, is granted hereby under any patents, copyrights or other intellectual property rights of peterfgallagher.com and a2B.consulting or others.

The document contains statements that are general in nature and do not constitute recommendations to the reader as to the content's suitability, applicability or appropriateness.

PFG Publishing has no responsibility for the persistence or accuracy of URLs for external or third-party internet websites referred to in this publication and does not guarantee that any content on such websites is, or will remain, accurate or appropriate.

Dedication

I dedicate this book to my wife Sarah and son Tiarnán, who I love and treasure.

Acknowledgements

In a career that spans over thirty years, I've worked for some wonderful people in many great locations, both onshore and offshore. There was never a dull moment. You have helped me learn so much and for that I am very grateful.

I would like to thank the brilliant people that I have had the good fortune to meet, work with and learn from. In a small way, each experience contributes and has helped me to write this book.

Never give up, judge or criticise, and always learn, improve, and love.

How this Book is Structured

All too often, change management implementations fail to deliver the expected organisation benefits or gain employee adoption. **Change Management Adoption - Leadership of Change® Volume 5** is aimed at an organisation's leaders of change and anyone involved or wanting to learn more about practical change management adoption. The book has four main sections:

Section 1 - Change Management Introduction: This section introduces the key change concepts that are considered a necessary foundation for leaders of change. It refers to change disruption, benefits realisation, organisational change challenges, change leadership, sponsorship, etc.

Section 2 - Change Management Framework and Models: This section includes the framework which supports programme change delivery. It also includes change models for leadership, sponsorship and behaviour. All the models are aligned with the **a2B Change Management Framework® (a2BCMF®)**.

Section 3 - AUILM® Employee Change Adoption Model: This is the core section of the book and outlines in detail how to support employees through the change transition by providing **A**wareness, **U**nderstanding, **I**nvolvement, **L**earning, and **M**otivation (**AUILM®**) for the change. At the end of **Sections 3.1, 3.2, 3.3, 3.4** and **3.5** a table will refer to key concepts that are structured within the **a2B Change Management Framework®** (see Volume 3).

Section 4 - Support Information: This section contains a detailed change management glossary and other reference information.

Who is this Leadership of Change® book for?

Change Management Adoption Volume 5 is targeted at all change management professionals and anyone responsible for implementing their organisation's change, with a focus on employee change adoption. This book will also be of interest to change practitioners, HR professionals, students studying change management, and project managers, including organisational managers and leaders.

Preface

For the last thirty years, I have worked in over thirty countries, across aerospace, defence, energy, finance, manufacturing, mining and pensions. I have been both an internal and external consultant. My work has covered manufacturing, quality, lean six sigma initiatives, operational excellence, ERP implementations, CEO special projects, major organisational change and transformations.

Change Management has always fascinated and excited me, it is my passion and when you find your passion your work no longer feels like work. When I look back at the projects or programmes that were successful, they had strong change management and communication components. But the ones that stood out, and were really successful, those were the ones that had:

➢ An effective, proactive and engaging sponsor.

➢ Effective and proactive change leadership.

➢ An employee adoption or behavioural change element.

I have yet to encounter a successful change implementation without an effective and proactive sponsor, backed by an aligned leadership team with change leadership skills and knowledge.

My previous books contain the framework, models, tools and concepts which are the foundations on how to implement successful organisational change. The **Leadership of Change® Volume 5** outlines the five critical steps that all change professionals should follow to support their organisation's change management implementation with a focus on employee adoption, structured on the **AUILM® Employee Change Adoption Model**.

*When focusing on employee change adoption, there are five key life cycle steps that all change professionals should follow to support their organisation's change management implementation, structured on the **AUILM® Employee Change Adoption Model***

Contents

Leadership of Change®	iv
Change Management Adoption	v
Copyright ©	vi
Disclaimer	vii
Dedication	viii
Acknowledgements	ix
How this Book is Structured	x
Preface	xi
Contents	xii
List of Figures and Tables	xvi
Section 1: Introduction	1
1.1 Change Adoption is Not a Single Solution	2
1.2 Change Disruption	4
1.3 Change Management	6
1.4 Organisational Change Challenges	8
1.5 Benefits of Change Management	12
1.6 Change Management Leadership	14
1.7 Change Benefits Realisation	16
1.8 Change Management Sponsorship	18
1.9 Dealing with Fixed Mindset Leaders	20
Section 2: Change Management Framework and Models	23
2.1 a2B Change Management Framework®	24
2.1.1 a2B Change Management Framework® Icons	26

Contents

2.2 AMI® Change Leadership Model	28
2.3 a2B3S® Change Sponsorship Model	30
2.4 a2B5R® Employee Behaviour Change Model	32

Section 3: AUILM® Employee Change Adoption Model — 34

3.0.1 AUILM® Employee Change Adoption Model	35
3.0.2 AUILM® Employee Change Adoption Model - Icons	36
3.0.3 AUILM® Model Overview	38
3.0.4 Organisation Change Alignment	42
3.0.5 Employee Support and Alignment	44
3.0.6 Process Alignment	46
3.0.7 Systems Alignment	48
3.0.8 Leadership Alignment	50

Section 3.1: Awareness - Plan Phase — 52

3.1.0 AUILM®: Awareness Overview	54
3.1.1 Employee: What's In It For Me (WIIFM)?	58
3.1.2 Processes: Creating Process Change Awareness	59
3.1.3 Systems: Creating System Change Awareness	60
3.1.4 Leadership: Creating Change Vision Awareness	61
3.1.5 a2BCMF® Step 1.1 Change Capacity	62
3.1.6 a2BCMF® Step 1.2 Change Elevator Speech	63
3.1.7 a2BCMF® Step 2.1 Sponsorship	64
3.1.8 a2BCMF® Step 2.2 Change Agents	65
3.1.9 a2B Change Management Framework® Steps 1 - 2	66

Section 3.2: Understanding - Plan Phase — 68

3.2.0 AUILM®: Understanding Overview	70
3.2.1 Employee: How Will this Change Impact Me?	74
3.2.2 Processes: Understand Why Processes Change	75
3.2.3 Systems: Understand Why Systems Change	76

3.2.4 Leadership: Creating Change Vision Understanding	77
3.2.5 a2BCMF® Step 3.1 Organisation Structure	78
3.2.6 a2BCMF® Step 3.2 Organisation Workload	79
3.2.7 a2BCMF® Step 4.1 Learning Plan	80
3.2.8 a2BCMF® Step 4.2 Resistance Strategy Plan (RSP)	81
3.2.9 a2B Change Management Framework® Steps 3 - 4	82

Section 3.3: Involvement - Execute Phase — 84

3.3.0 AUILM®: Involvement Overview	86
3.3.1 Employee: Will I Be Involved?	90
3.3.2 Processes: Process Improvement Involvement	91
3.3.3 Systems: System Improvement Involvement	92
3.3.4 Leadership: Involved and Modelling the New Way	93
3.3.5 a2BCMF® Step 5.1 Employee 1:1s	94
3.3.6 a2BCMF® Step 5.2 Change Design Workshops	95
3.3.7 a2BCMF® Step 6.1 Governance	96
3.3.8 a2BCMF® Step 6.2 Culture	97
3.3.9 a2B Change Management Framework® Steps 5 - 6	98

Section 3.4: Learning - Execute Phase — 100

3.4.0 AUILM®: Learning Overview	102
3.4.1 Employee: Learning the New Skills and Behaviours	106
3.4.2 Processes: Learning the New Processes	107
3.4.3 Systems: Learning the New Systems	108
3.4.4 Leadership: Learning and Modelling the New Way	109
3.4.5 a2BCMF® Step 7.1 Resistance Tipping Point	110
3.4.6 a2BCMF® Step 7.2 Implementation Approaches	111
3.4.7 a2BCMF® Step 8.1 Develop New Skills	112
3.4.8 a2BCMF® Step 8.2 Develop New Behaviours	113
3.4.9 a2B Change Management Framework® Steps 7 - 8	114

Section 3.5: Motivation - Sustain Phase   116

   3.5.0 AUILM®: Motivation Overview   118

   3.5.1 Employee: What Will keep Me Motivated?   122

   3.5.2 Processes: Motivate to Ensure Process Adherence   123

   3.5.3 Systems: Motivate to Ensure System Compliance   124

   3.5.4 Leadership: Motivating and Intervening   125

   3.5.5 a2BCMF® Step 9.1 Change Adoption Assessment   126

   3.5.6 a2BCMF® Step 9.2 Growth Mindset   127

   3.5.7 a2BCMF® Step 10.1 Sustain the Change   128

   3.5.8 a2BCMF® Step 10.2 Close the Change Programme   129

   3.5.9 a2B Change Management Framework® Steps 9 - 10   130

Section 4: Support Information   132

   4.1 Glossary   133

   4.2 Afterword   146

   4.3 About the Author   147

   4.4 Other Leadership of Change® Volumes   148

   4.5 Connect with Me Online   150

List of Figures and Tables

Figure 1.1 Leadership of Change® Approaches	3
Figure 1.2 Industrial Revolutions	5
Figure 1.3 Change Management Definition	6
Figure 1.4 Organisational Change Management Challenges	10
Figure 1.5 Change Management Benefit Realisation	13
Figure 2.1 a2B Change Management Framework®	24
Figure 2.2 AMI® Change Leadership Model	28
Figure 2.3. a2B3S® Change Sponsorship Model	30
Figure 2.4 a2B5R® Employee Behaviour Change Model	32
Figure 3.0.1 AUILM® Employee Change Adoption Model	35
Figure 3.0.3 Employee Change Transition Support	39
Figure 3.0.4 Change Adoption Organisation Alignment	42
Figure 3.1 AUILM® Model - Awareness	53
Figure 3.1.5 Estimated Organisation Capacity for Change	62
Figure 3.1.6 Change Elevator Speech	63
Figure 3.1.7 Key Elements of Sponsorship	64
Figure 3.1.8 Change Agents - Internal Versus External	65
Figure 3.1.9 Change Management Framework® Steps 1 - 2	66
Table 3.1.10 Step 1 - 2 a2BCMF® Change Considerations	67
Figure 3.2 AUILM® Model - Understanding	69
Figure 3.2.9 Change Management Framework® Steps 3 - 4	82
Table 3.2.10 Step 3 - 4 a2BCMF® Change Considerations	83
Figure 3.3 AUILM® Model - Involvement	85

List of Figures and Tables

Figure 3.3.9 Change Management Framework® Steps 5 - 6	98
Table 3.3.10 Steps 5 - 6 a2BCMF® Change Considerations	99
Figure 3.4 AUILM® Model - Learning	101
Figure 3.4.5 Change Resistance Standpoints	110
Figure 3.4.6 Change Implementation Approaches	111
Figure 3.4.7 Develop New Skills	112
Figure 3.4.8 Develop New Behaviours	113
Figure 3.4.9 Change Management Framework® Steps 7 - 8	114
Table 3.4.10 Step 7 - 8 a2BCMF® Change Considerations	115
Figure 3.5 AUILM® Model - Motivation	117
Figure 3.5.5 AUILM® Change Adoption Assessment	126
Figure 3.5.6 Fixed versus Growth Mindset	127
Figure 3.5.7 Sustain the Change	128
Figure 3.5.8 Close the Change Programme	129
Figure 3.5.9 Change Management Framework® Steps 9 - 10	130
Table 3.5.10 Step 9 - 10 a2BCMF® Change Considerations	131

Section 1: Introduction

1.1 Change Adoption is Not a Single Solution

Any change professional who thinks they can implement successful organisation change solely with a change adoption model would be better equipped to cross the Atlantic in a rowing boat

Achieving employee change adoption in a major organisation change or transformation has mixed success. For change adoption to be successful, the leaders, sponsor and change team should support employees through the change transition by providing **A**wareness, **U**nderstanding, **I**nvolvement, **L**earning, and **M**otivation for the change. The **AUILM® Employee Change Adoption Model** supports this change transition.

However, a pure change adoption approach fundamentally misses other change programme delivery success elements (**Figure 1.1**). If these elements are missing, it will be nearly impossible to deliver employee adoption and successful change. These key elements are:

> **a2B Change Management Framework® (a2BCMF®)**: A structured and disciplined approach to support organisations, leadership teams and individuals going through a change, the transition from the current state '**a**' to the improved future state '**B**'. It has ten key steps but iterations between the steps are usually necessary and some can be worked in parallel. It supports change programme delivery, from ensuring the change is aligned to the organisation's strategy through to officially closing the programme.

> **Change Management Leadership**: Effective and proactive leadership is essential for successful organisational change. Leaders have three critical responsibilities: **A**rticulate the vision, **M**odel the new way and **I**ntervene to ensure sustainable change. These responsibilities are structured on the **AMI® Change**

Leadership Model. If the leaders are focused on other activities, there is little chance the change programme will get the resources or attention it needs to ensure successful employee change adoption.

Leadership of Change® Approaches

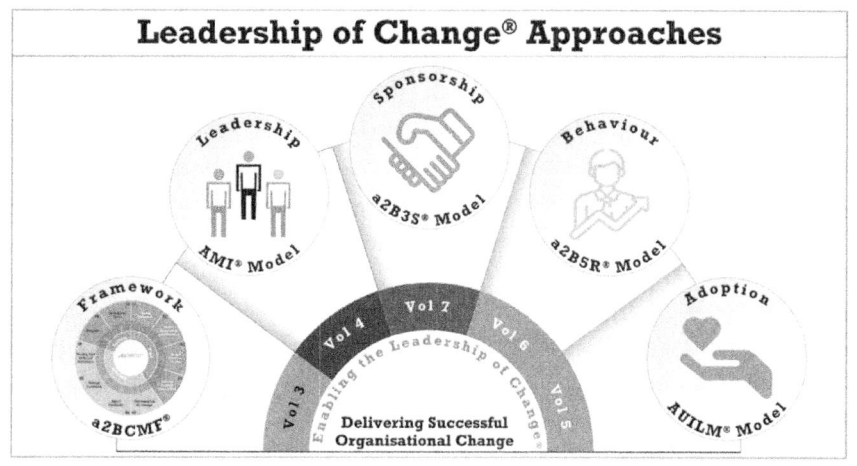

Figure 1.1 Leadership of Change® Approaches

> **Change Management Sponsorship**: The sponsor has three critical responsibilities to implement successful change: **Say** - communicate the change, **Support** - provide resources and **Sustain** - embed the change. These responsibilities are structured on the **a2B3S® Change Sponsorship Model**. Without an effective and proactive change sponsor, the change team is unlikely to get resources, the right access to impacted stakeholders, organisation agenda time, etc. Without these, most change programmes fail to achieve employee adoption.

> **Change Management Behaviour**: In order for an organisation to successfully deliver sustainable employee change adoption and benefits realisation, some type of employee behaviour change is usually required. To change these behaviours, the organisation must support employees through the change transition by implementing five key life cycle steps: **Recognise**, **Redesign**, **Resolve**, **Replicate** and **Reinforce**. The **a2B5R® Employee Behaviour Change Model** supports this change transition.

1.2 Change Disruption

Change disruption is the order of the day. Rapidly changing customer buying habits, access to new technology, and social media accelerate the way organisations need to adapt to change to remain competitive or even survive

The first industrial revolution in the eighteenth-century allowed production to be mechanised. This revolution drove social change as people became increasingly urbanised. The second industrial revolution developed mass production, and the third, beginning in the 1950s, saw the emergence of computers and digital technology. This led to increased automation through digitisation and computers.

We are currently in the middle of the fourth industrial revolution (4IR) and a time of major disruption (**Figure 1.2**). 4IR is differentiated by the speed of technological breakthroughs and its widespread scope. It has had an incredible impact, changing the way organisations operate and how we live and relate to one another. 4IR includes technology breakthroughs in fields such as artificial intelligence, robotics, the Internet of Things, autonomous vehicles, 3D printing, 5G, genetic modification and energy storage. 4IR will impact the workforce like never before, it will radically change how we get to work, where we work, what we work on and how we work.

At its core, the fourth industrial revolution has brought forth four main challenges to business:

> **Customer Expectations**: Customers are more important than ever, they also have more knowledge and choice. To remain competitive, organisations will have to respond to customers quickly, with more flexibility, transparency, and customisation.
> **Product and Service Enhancement**: Innovation, new technology and digital advancements will transform products and

services. They will be given additional capabilities, their value will increase, they will become more durable, easier to service, etc.
- **Collaborative Innovation**: Apart from tech giants, few organisations will have the multiple types of expertise required to maximise their potential. More collaboration and partnerships will be required, not just between vendors but also internationally.
- **Business Operating Models**: Organisational structures and operational models will need to constantly change and adapt to enable them to leverage ongoing technology developments. Organisations will need talent strategies to attract and retain talent, as well as deliver continuous learning.

Industrial Revolutions

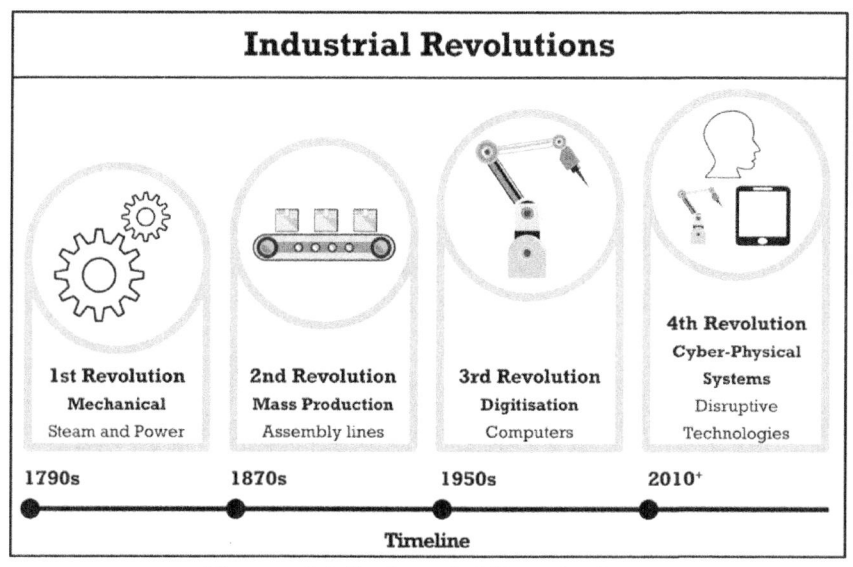

1st Revolution	2nd Revolution	3rd Revolution	4th Revolution
Mechanical	Mass Production	Digitisation	Cyber-Physical Systems
Steam and Power	Assembly lines	Computers	Disruptive Technologies
1790s	1870s	1950s	2010+

Timeline

Figure 1.2 Industrial Revolutions

Change will impact nearly every organisation like an explosion, continually disrupting how the organisation delivers normal day-to-day operations. How organisations react to this change will become a source of competitive advantage. Their ability to reduce the internal period of disruption and negative performance to deliver positive operating performance and future state benefits will be critical. 4IR will ensure that organisational change is going to be a part of doing business but what if we could embrace change and lead the world through the **Leadership of Change®**?

1.3 Change Management

Change management is the process, techniques and tools to support organisations, leadership teams and employees going through a change transition from the current 'a' state to the improved future 'B' state

Organisational change management has evolved over the last few decades, previously taking the form of communications and last-minute training just before a new change was implemented, and covering the softer aspects of people management. At that point in time, change management was a fragmented activity, a tick box exercise on the project plan with no obvious link to project success or measurable results.

Leadership of Change® - Change Management Definition
Change management is the process, techniques and tools to support organisations, leadership teams and employees going through a change transition from the current 'a' state to the improved future 'B' state. It minimises organisation disruption and maximises benefits

Figure 1.3 Change Management Definition

Today, in times of change disruption, change management is seen by leading organisations as critical strategic capability. It will enable an organisation to keep ahead of their competition or potentially even help them to survive. An organisation's strategic portfolio sets out multiple programmes and projects that need to be implemented to meet changing customer requirements, stay ahead of the competition, utilise new technology, etc. But, in order to adapt and reap the benefits of the new technology, we need employees to change and adopt the new way of working. Change management is the enabler (**Figure 1.3**).

The objective of change management is to minimise organisation disruption (any impact on day-to-day operations and growing change resistance) and maximise organisation benefits (employee adoption and improved operating performance). Change management specifically helps employees to become aware of the change, to understand the business needs, become involved, and develop the new skills and behaviours so they can adopt the new way of working. It also motivates employees to commit to sustaining the change, ensuring the organisation achieves its benefits and return on investment.

Key Focuses of Change Management Implementation

The **Leadership of Change**® focuses on the three basics of organisational change implementation:

1. **Programme Change Delivery**:
   - **A Change Management Framework**: A disciplined and structured programme approach to deliver business change.
   - **Change Processes, Tools and Techniques**: Important change concepts used while driving and delivering change.
   - **Change Capability**: Employees with verifiable change management skills and knowledge to deliver successful change.

2. **Employee Change Support**:
   - **Change Adoption Support**: Change success is highly dependent on employees adopting the new way of working and they should be supported through the change transition to achieve adoption.
   - **Behaviour Change Support**: Behavioural change is often critical to change success. Employees should be supported to develop the new behaviours.

3. **Organisational Change Alignment**:
   - **Leadership**: Leaders lead the change, this is fundamental to change success because of their position and influence in the organisation.
   - **Organisational Structure Alignment**: The structure of the organisation, its business processes and systems must be aligned with the employees and leaders, supported by the sponsor.
   - **Sponsorship**: A leader with overall responsibility for delivering the change programme on behalf of the organisation.

1.4 Organisational Change Challenges

There are many challenges that organisations consistently face when implementing change, such as leadership alignment, normal day-to-day operations, and organisation change capability

Lots of statistics show organisational change and transformations failing to deliver their intended benefits. You can argue about the true percentage of success, but the fact is that many organisations do not achieve full benefits realisation, and in many cases, they fail to attain a return on investment (ROI). Equally unacceptable to shareholders is that the vision is not realised, meaning the organisation's strategy has not been executed. Even when the organisation and its leadership team agree the changes are necessary for the future of the organisation, they still face a number of consistent and specific challenges (**Figure 1.4**). The challenges of implementing organisational change start with competing with normal day-to-day operations, they also include leadership alignment, resistance to change adoption and/or behaviour change, as well as having change capability to get the implementation approach right.

There will be many challenges and barriers for organisations. These can be listed in two categories: consistent challenges throughout change implementation, and specific challenges throughout change implementation.

Consistent Challenges Throughout Change Implementation:

➢ **Normal Day-to-Day Operations**: Balancing urgent daily operational activities that need to be completed against important strategic change management activities.

- **Leadership**: Leaders not fully supporting the change in terms of their responsibilities: **A̲rticulate** the change vision, **M̲odel** the new behaviours and **I̲ntervene** to reinforce the change.
- **Organisation Change Capability**: Organisations constantly facing change recognise they need to use internal capabilities and have a standard approach, a change framework, models, processes and tools.

Specific Challenges Throughout Change Implementation:

- **Too Many Change Initiatives**: Not enough capacity to deliver ongoing and new change programmes.
- **Inactive or Invisible Sponsorship**: Lack of visible support usually leads to change failure.
- **Poor Previous Change History**: This increases the likelihood of repeating past mistakes.
- **No Detailed Project Change Plan**: Implementing change with only a communication plan and not aligning it to the master project plan.
- **Poor Communication**: Lack of employee engagement and communication.
- **Ignoring Change Readiness Input**: If the change readiness assessment indicates the organisation is not ready then the change should not be implemented.
- **Thinking there is N̲o Resistance**: There will always be resistance, even if it is not overt!
- **Ignoring the Importance of Behaviours**: If you do not change employee behaviour, you will not get organisational change.
- **Thinking Employees will Adopt the Change**: Employees will need to be supported throughout the change by the leadership team, so adoption is maximised.
- **Not Transferring Ownership**: Not closing the change properly by using a structured process to ensure sustainment and benefits delivery.

Organisational Change

Plan — Get the organisation ready

⚠ Too many Change Initiatives

⚠ Inactive and Invisible Sponsorship

1. Change Definition
2. Sponsorship and Resources

⚠ Ignoring the Importance of Behaviours

⚠ Thinking there is No Resistance

8. Develop New Skills and Behaviours
7. Manage Resistance

Sustain — Adoption and benefits realisation

⚠ Thinking Employees will Adopt Change

⚠ Not Transferring Ownership

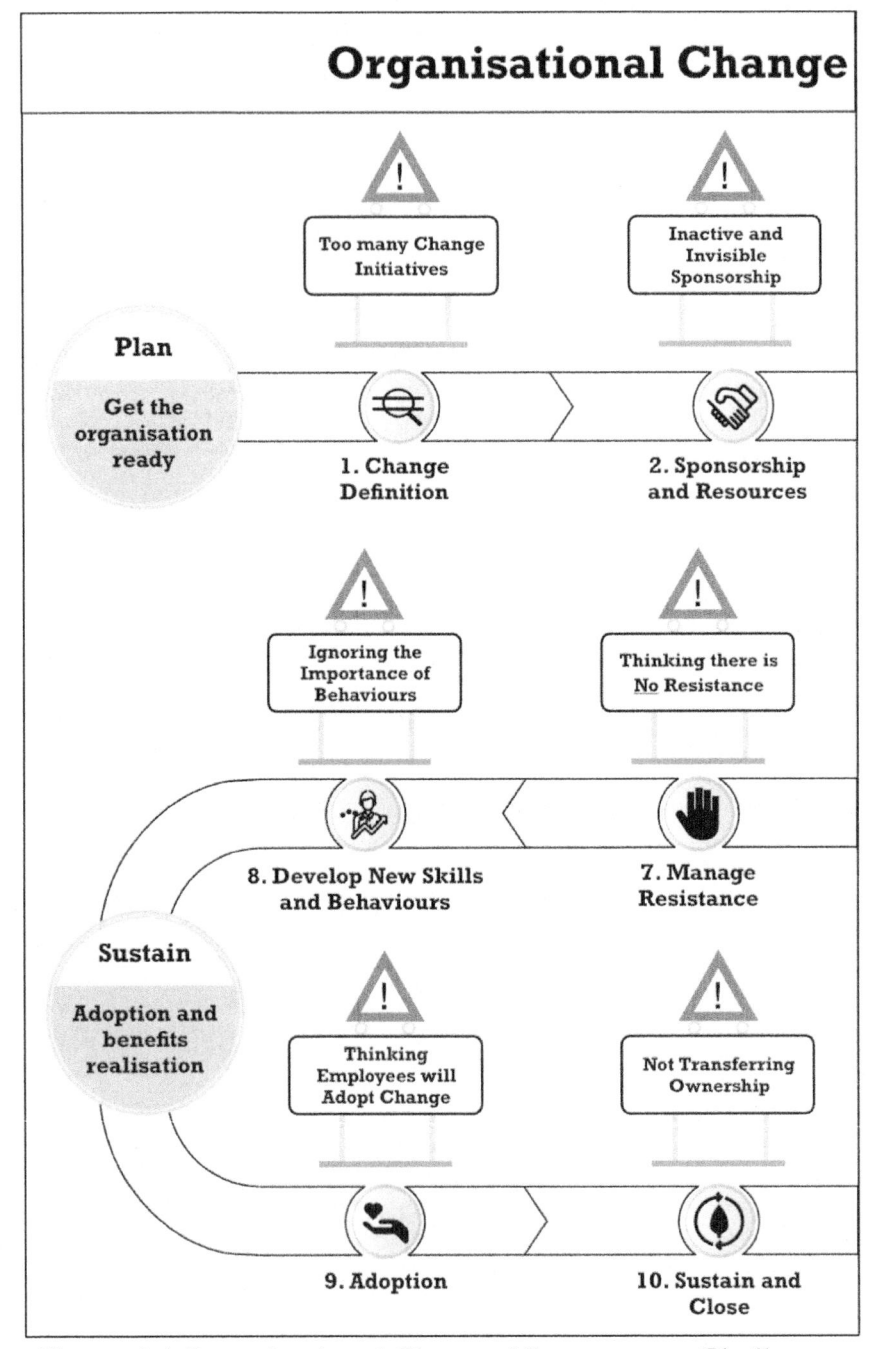

9. Adoption
10. Sustain and Close

Figure 1.4 Organisational Change Management Challenges

1.4 Organisational Change Challenges

Management Challenges

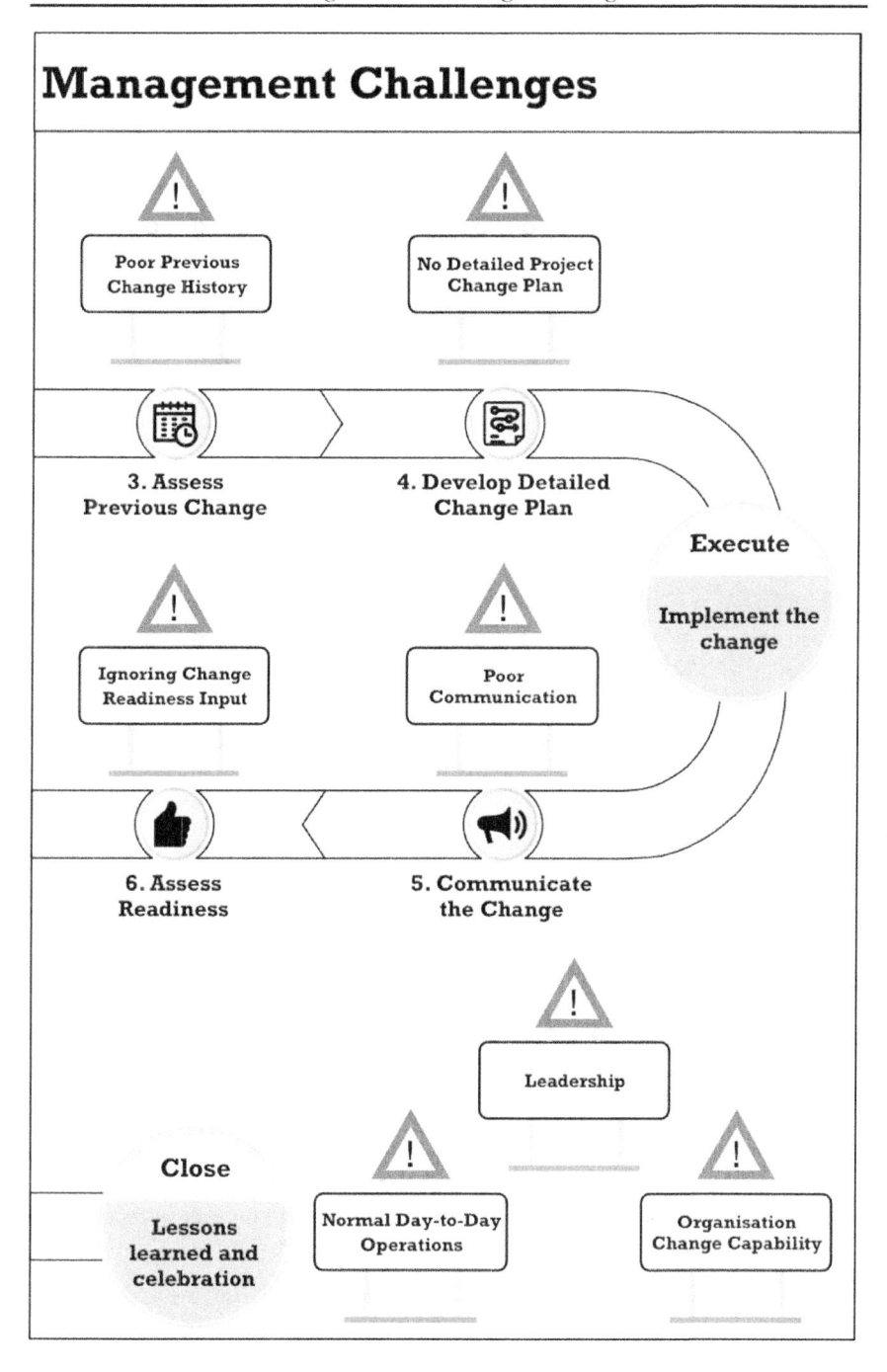

- Poor Previous Change History
- No Detailed Project Change Plan

3. Assess Previous Change
4. Develop Detailed Change Plan

Execute — Implement the change

- Ignoring Change Readiness Input
- Poor Communication

6. Assess Readiness
5. Communicate the Change

Close — Lessons learned and celebration

- Leadership
- Normal Day-to-Day Operations
- Organisation Change Capability

11

1.5 Benefits of Change Management

While change programmes focus on strategy execution to improve organisation performance, shareholders, at a minimum, expect benefits delivery

Too many organisational change, improvement, and transformation programmes fail, which means that objectives are not achieved, and the organisation fails to execute their strategy. These failed change attempts do not usually have a planned and systematic approach to preparing, communicating, and implementing change into the organisation. The key to the effective implementation of change programmes is to develop and deploy structured approaches that will help organisations, leaders, teams and employees understand, accept and work with change, to minimise resistance and disruption. The main benefits of using a structured approach to change management are to deliver successful change and meet targets:

- Time.
- Budget.
- Scope.
- Change Implementation.
- Improved Business Performance.

Benefits Realisation and Period of Disruption

There are three potential approaches that organisations and their leaders can choose (**Figure 1.5**):

- **Unmanaged Change - High Disruption - Low Benefits**: With unmanaged change, the organisation's leaders push the change into the organisation but continue to focus on normal day-to-day operations. This usually results in a long period of disruption to

1.5 Benefits of Change Management

the organisation, negative performance, low benefits realisation and a failure to get a return on investment.

➢ **Reactive Change - Medium Disruption - Medium Benefits**: With reactive change, the organisation's leaders push the change into the organisation but keep both a focus on normal day-to-day operations and on the change. They react to poor implementation progress by moving some of their people onto the change. This usually results in medium disruption, medium benefits realisation and a small improvement in operating performance.

➢ **Supported Change - Low Disruption - High Benefits**: With supported change, the organisation's leaders push the change into the organisation, agreeing that the success of this change is important to ensure the organisation's strategy is executed. They understand that today's operations provide revenue for now, but the successful implementation of the change will ensure revenue for tomorrow. So, they assign some of their best people to lead the change whilst leaving others to focus on operations. This usually results in a shorter period of disruption, higher future performance and benefits realisation, and a return on investment.

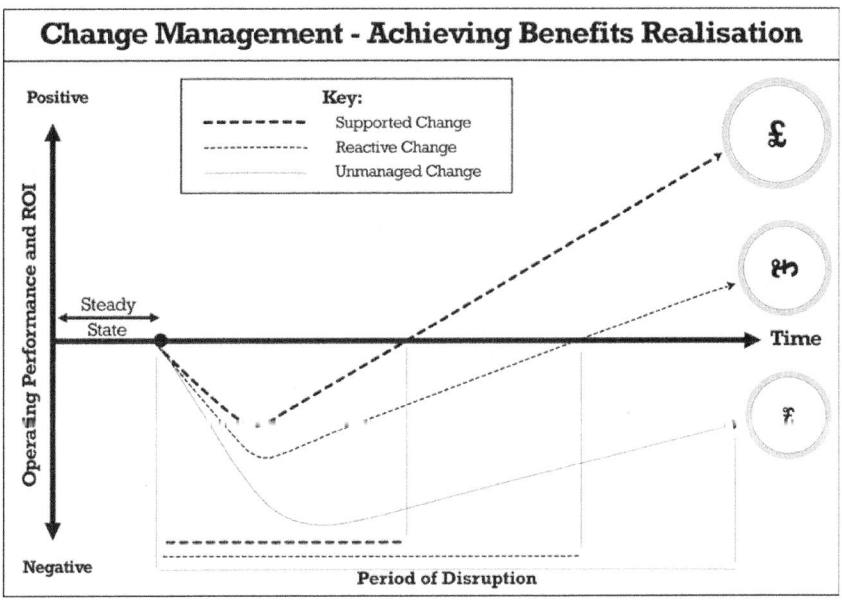

Figure 1.5 Change Management Benefit Realisation

1.6 Change Management Leadership

*Organisational change leadership is about effectively and proactively **A**rticulating the vision, **M**odelling the new way and **I**ntervening to ensure sustainable change*

Effective and proactive leadership is essential for successful organisational change. Leaders go about their daily task of implementing the organisation's strategy to deliver financial results, when all of a sudden there is a change explosion that disrupts operations and results. They face the leadership paradox: implementing change versus delivering day-to-day operations. Leaders then need to adjust their focus to implement the change, so that the organisation stays ahead of the competition and continues to deliver revenue to its shareholders. That means the change has to ensure a return on investment (ROI), full employee change adoption, and sustainable change.

The technology revolution shows no sign of slowing, and future leaders will have to be equally skilled at simultaneously leading operations and change implementation. Until recently, an organisational leader or manager could just focus on normal day-to-day operations, handing off change management and implementation responsibilities to other people. Their responsibility was to approve the budget, send an email announcing the programme, and confirm who they had made accountable for delivery. Unfortunately, they kept their best people around them to support day-to-day operations, with the change programme being run by people who were 'available' at the time. No consideration was given as to why those people were available, nor to the longer-term missed opportunity of not putting the best people on the organisation's key strategic investment for future success.

The days when a leader could announce a new change programme by email with an attached presentation are numbered. The PowerPoint presentation may cover the change objectives, timelines, and business case, but it is a one-way communication tool that does not check for employee understanding, nor does it collect feedback. It is too late to wait until the technology implementation goes live and fails before the leader intervenes. By this point the damage may be done, and the situation may not be recoverable. Even if it is recoverable, there will be delays in implementation, user adoption rates might be lower than planned, and the ROI may never be fully realised. There is also the damage to reputation, employee resistance might have grown, and the success of future change could be tarnished.

Organisational change management, transformation, and improvement have become permanent features of the business landscape. The owners and shareholders of organisations are now starting to demand that the leaders they select have both day-to-day operational and change implementation skills. The leader of change needs to go well beyond sending out an email. They need to ensure that the change is aligned with strategy and that they support the sponsor, engage and communicate with employees to reduce resistance, support user adoption, and ensure sustainable benefits. It is critical that leaders engage all levels of the organisation to ensure that both the organisation and the employees have capacity for the change. Change comes so constantly and quickly that if leaders don't focus on properly balancing today's normal day-to-day operations with change implementation, there may be no day-to-day operations tomorrow. Leaders must get today's changes right.

Leading change can be one of the most difficult burdens of a leader's role, especially when normal day-to-day operations continually throw up urgent activities that must be dealt with. Effective and proactive leadership is essential for successful change and organisations with this capability will have a competitive advantage, helping them to stay ahead in the marketplace.

The three critical leader responsibilities for the successful leadership of change are **Articulate**, **Model** and **Intervene**. **Section 2.2** introduces the **AMI® Change Leadership Model** and further understanding can be found in **Change Management Leadership - Leadership of Change® Volume 4**.

1.7 Change Benefits Realisation

It never ceases to amaze me how often I have to remind change management professionals that the reason we are implementing the change is to achieve benefits realisation

The reason that organisations have change programmes and invest time, resources, money and effort is to realise benefits and add value to the organisation. Benefits realisation is an integral part of change management, but it is often overlooked or becomes less of a priority when the change team is distracted by other urgent activities in delivering the change. Each organisation will have its own inherent processes for benefits realisation and in some change programmes a finance professional may join the team to have accountability for this activity. Whatever the agreed process, the objective is to successfully deliver quantifiable and meaningful business benefits to the organisation. Benefits realisation includes the following processes:

> **Identification**: Identify, quantify and qualify the business benefits or value to the organisation. Identification should start at the portfolio level and be developed through the completion of the business case.

> **Analysis and Planning**: This stage will normally require input from other functions within the organisation, and the analysis and planning can become very detailed, depending on the value of the change programme. This will probably include establishing measures or metrics, a baseline and schedule, as well as potential and associated risks.

- **Delivery**: Depending on the type of change programme, the benefits can either start to happen during the Execute phase or after the change is implemented and the programme closes. Either way, there should be a benefits delivery schedule to track estimated savings against actual savings. However, it should be noted that not all change programmes have direct savings, sometimes benefits are intangible or focus on avoiding costs that would otherwise be incurred, etc.

- **Sustainment**: One of the biggest challenges of any change programme is how the benefits will be sustained long after the change team has moved on. The four key elements of Sustain are:
  - **Benefits Delivery Transition and Sustainment**: Establishing a responsible party after the change team has dissolved to track and monitor benefits.
  - **Balanced Scorecard (BSC)**: Linking the change benefits realisation to specific organisation performance measures.
  - **Individual Performance Plan (IPP)**: Aligning employee performance to benefits realisation to support change success. This is covered in more detail in **a2BCMF® Step 10 - Sustain and Close**.
  - **Adoption**: Without full employee adoption of the new way of working it is unlikely the change will realise the benefits targeted in this step. This is covered in more detail in **a2BCMF® Step 9 - Adoption**.

Benefits Plan and Tracker - Insights:

- The benefits plan and tracker is a document detailing the planned benefits of the change and on-going progress. Depending on the magnitude of the benefits, the benefits plan and tracker can become complex to include monthly or quarterly columns for comparing estimated budget spend versus actual, mitigation plans, etc.

- If the benefits of the change programme are not properly articulated or communicated, they will not receive the attention of the organisation or stakeholder support and will most likely fail.

1.8 Change Management Sponsorship

Without effective and proactive sponsorship, the change programme will eventually fail, the change will not be adopted by the employees or sustained, and it will not deliver the intended benefits

The sponsor is authorised to mandate the programme and the business case, and is responsible for change adoption, benefits realisation and successful change programme delivery. Simply put, without an effective and proactive change sponsor, most change programmes or initiatives will fail to achieve the targeted objectives. To be effective, the sponsor will need to have a good team behind them, fully supported by the organisation's leadership team. The team will need to be dedicated, motivated with a strong understanding of people, and have good change and communication skills. As with all change programmes and general projects, they are a temporary endeavour, and acquiring and developing the sponsor and change resources is a critical success factor. However, accepting a resource that is 'available' could be more problematic than you might think.

The sponsor acts as the representative of the organisation and is primarily concerned with ensuring that the change programme delivers the agreed upon business benefits. They play a vital leadership role and the bigger the change programme, the more senior the sponsor should be. The sponsor is not just a figurehead role, and the position will vary from organisation to organisation. The sponsor does not need to have project management skills, but they should understand the basics, such as the triple constraint; time, cost and scope. The sponsor should also be ready to cancel the change programme, either because its charter is fulfilled or conditions arise that bring the programme to an early close, such as the change is no longer aligned with the organisation's strategy.

1.8 Change Management Sponsorship

A distinction must be made between sponsorship and leadership. Change management sponsorship is different from leadership and is much more important in terms of delivering and implementing successful organisational change. In terms of change management, the sponsor's task is to successfully deliver organisational change, but this cannot be achieved without the full support of the organisation's leaders who **Articulate** the change vision, **Model** the new behaviours and **Intervene** to reinforce the change (**see Section 2.2**). **Section 2.3** outlines the three main sponsor responsibilities, **Say**, **Support** and **Sustain** (**Figure 2.3**).

Sponsor activities may include:

- Leadership alignment.
- Programme governance.
- Financial control and oversight.
- Intervening with other leaders to ensure competent change resources are released from day-to-day operations to the change programme.
- Developing internal change capability.
- Risk management.
- Change deliverables progress and approval.
- Approving communications.
- Engaging, arbitrating and mediating between impacted stakeholders.

1.9 Dealing with Fixed Mindset Leaders

Fixed mindset leaders will quickly contaminate an organisation by killing growth and creativity, as well as promoting incompetence based on their likeness. This cycle will be replicated unless shareholders intervene ruthlessly

According to Niccolò Machiavelli, *"It must be remembered that there is nothing more difficult to plan, more doubtful of success, nor more dangerous to manage than a new system. For the initiator has the enmity of all who would profit by the preservation of the old institution and merely lukewarm defenders in those who gain by the new ones."* If, as a change professional, you start the process of implementing meaningful change into your organisation and this makes some leaders uncomfortable, you could be seen as a threat to them, making you a target in many ways.

It is a fallacy to think that only employees who have something to lose will resist change, and that the senior leaders of an organisation will not resist because they 'should' be executing the organisation's strategy. In some cases, the leaders of the organisation have got much more to lose, in terms of position, status and salary. They will have asked themselves, 'What's In It For Me?' (WIIFM) and if the answer is not favourable, they could overtly work against the change, especially those trying to implement it.

It is typical for change professionals to hear, *"It is not us, it is the employees below me that have the problem with change and improvement"* when engaging with organisational leaders at the start of a change journey. One cannot be sure if this organisational change challenge is due to fixed mindset and deluded leaders or the sheep that follow them in abundance.

> ➤ **Fixed Mindset Leaders**: Tend to put their own needs above the needs of the organisation and their fellow employees, remaining loyal to the old ways. They are unable to see or admit that they are a major barrier to successful change. The toxic consequence is that

1.8 Dealing with Fixed Mindset Leaders

fixed mindset leaders have already been promoted based on this mindset, and this behaviour has therefore been reinforced, to the detriment of the organisation. Typically, these behaviours will be emulated by their direct reports because they have been perceived as successful leadership traits. Unfortunately, fixed mindset employees are often promoted based purely on their likeness to the leader and these inherent negative behaviours which are counterproductive to a successful organisation. They will contaminate the organisation's future, unless external and ruthless intervention is executed. Nothing will undermine change success more than leaders not role modelling the new mindset and behaviours.

➢ **Growth Mindset Leaders**: Embrace disruption and change, seeing it as an opportunity to improve organisation performance. There will be challenges ahead, mistakes will be made, but this adds to the exciting journey of continual learning, development and trying new things to keep ahead of the competition. Growth mindset leaders support the sponsor, communicate and lead the organisation and its employees through the change. They are the behavioural and cultural architects of change. Leadership teams play a critical role in making change successful, as they have a unique and powerful role in the organisation. Their role is to translate the vision of change from the CEO through to the employees whilst ensuring the department managers communicate the same consistent message. They will coach the new mindset and behaviours that are needed to make the change successful. Growth mindset leaders are successful because they are not afraid to fail, they learn and lead by example.

If you are going to be filling the position of a change professional and you are satisfied with comfortable change inaction, then a very high number of organisational leaders will welcome your approach. Unfortunately, this superficial approach is unlikely to achieve sustainable organisation change and benefits realisation. However, if you have a true passion for implementing organisational change, supporting employees to adopt change, and are prepared to call out a few organisational leaders who are not effective and proactive about the change you are involved in, it could be a fantastic, exiting and fulfilling journey.

Section 2: Change Management Framework and Models

2.1 a2B Change Management Framework®

a2B Change Management Framework®

3 main programme delivery phases — 10 steps tailored to suit each client

- 01 Change Definition
- 02 Secure Sponsorship and Resources
- 03 Assess Previous Change
- 04 Develop Detailed Change Plan
- 05 Communicate the Change
- 06 Assess Readiness
- 07 Manage Resistance
- 08 Develop New Skills and Behaviours
- 09 Adoption
- 10 Sustain and Close

Phases: Plan, Execute, Sustain — Enabling the Leadership of Change

Steps may have iterations — Strategy and leadership alignment

Figure 2.1 a2B Change Management Framework®

The a2B Change Management Framework® is a structured and disciplined programme approach to support organisations, leadership teams and employees going through a change

The **a2B Change Management Framework®** (**a2BCMF®**) is a structured and disciplined approach to support organisations, leadership teams and individuals going through a change, the transition from the current 'a' state to the improved future 'B' state (**Figure 2.1**). The **a2BCMF®** has three phases and ten key process steps. Each phase (Plan, Execute and Sustain) provides change strategies, principles, analysis and tactics to move from one phase to the next.

The framework is based on over thirty years of international change experience and brings together leading practice in change, people and programme management. The structured programme approach, processes, techniques and tools focus on overcoming the failures of previous change by incorporating ten key steps and success elements for achieving organisational change. It supports strategic change implementation in terms of context, content and process. The framework is a comprehensive management model that allows executives, managers and change practitioners to successfully deliver and achieve organisational change.

The **a2B Change Management Framework®** is a systematic approach to managing change within the organisation, whether it is change, transformation or the implementation of business improvement. All steps of the framework are interconnected, and the Execute and Sustain phases are driven by data from the change history assessment© (CHA©) performed during the Plan phase. It requires a holistic approach, and some steps can be performed simultaneously. The first **a2BCMF®** Step in the Plan phase ensures the change is aligned with the organisation's strategy and that it has been properly assessed as a business case that offers competitive advantage, value or benefits for the organisation. It asks, "What are the risks of doing the change?" and "Is there change capacity to implement the change while normal day-to-day operations continue?" The Execute phase covers communications, change readiness, resistance and developing the new skills and behaviours. The Sustain phase focuses on employee adoption and how the change should be sustained and officially closed. Finally, the framework aligns directly with the **AUILM® Employee Change Adoption Model (Figure 3.0.1)**, as well as the other **Leadership of Change®** models on leadership, sponsorship, and behaviour.

Main Benefits: The main benefits of using the **a2B Change Management Framework®** are to deliver successful sustainable change and meet targets:

- On time delivery.
- Achieve benefits realisation.
- Keep within scope.
- Change Implementation:
    - Achieve behavioural change.
    - Achieve change adoption.
- Improved business performance.

2.1.1 a2B Change Management Framework® Icons

	**Change Definition**: The process of defining the change and aligning the programmes within the portfolio to the organisation's strategy, ensuring it has a business case and resources to deliver business benefits.
	**Secure Sponsorship and Resources**: The process of identifying the sponsor and other change resources who will support the change during implementation.
	**Assess Previous Change**: The process of assessing previous change for future change management success, this involves analysing the organisation's change history to mitigate previous weaknesses and enhance future success.
	**Develop Detailed Change Plan**: The process of developing the Project Change Plan to document the actions, timelines, milestones and resources needed to deliver the programme. It should reference documents from **a2BCMF® Step 1** and may also include other component plans.
	**Communicate the Change**: The process of communicating the change simply and repeatedly with a feedback loop.

Assess Readiness: The process of assessing the change readiness of the organisation and the employees prior to change implementation.	
Manage Resistance: The process of managing inevitable resistance which is the negative reaction by the organisation or individuals when they perceive that a change coming their way could be a threat to them.	
Develop New Skills and Behaviours: The process of developing the new skills and knowledge, ensuring all impacted employees have the ability to perform their new role and they can role model the few new critical behaviours.	
Adoption: The process of leaving the old ways behind and adopting the new way of working, confirming the employees have fully accepted the change, in mind and heart.	
Sustain and Close: The process of sustaining and closing the change after the organisation and employees have adopted the change. Sustain and close should involve official approval within programme governance, including administration.	

2.2 AMI® Change Leadership Model

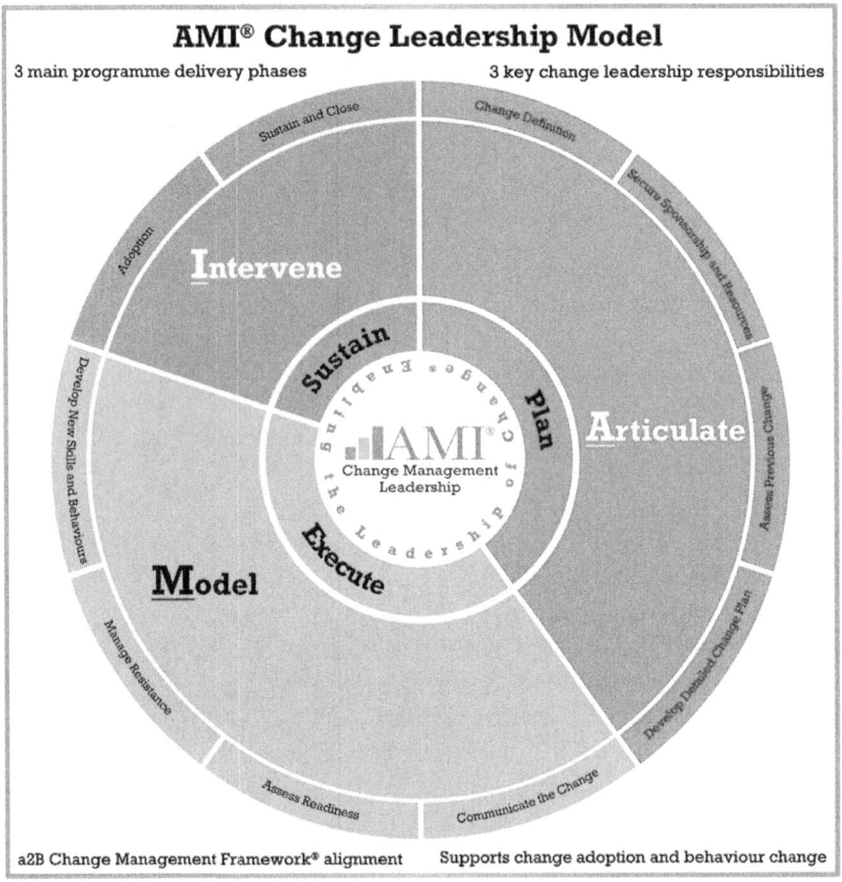

Figure 2.2 AMI® Change Leadership Model

Organisational change leadership is about effectively and proactively articulating the vision, modelling the new way and intervening to ensure sustainable change

Effective and proactive leadership is essential for successful organisational change. The **AMI® Change Leadership Model** (**Figure 2.2**) is a structured and disciplined approach for change management leaders to lead and support their organisation, department and team going through a change, the transition from the current '**a**' state to the improved future '**B**' state. The **AMI® Model** has three phases (Plan, Execute and Sustain) which provide change strategies, principles, analysis and tactics to move from one phase to the next. The three critical **Leadership of Change®** responsibilities are: **Articulate**, **Model** and **Intervene** to ensure sustainable change. These responsibilities of the change leader are then broken down into sub tasks and activities.

Corporate thinking about change leadership and change management has evolved in recent years and they are considered as core competences by some leading organisations. Varying degrees of change capability, low employee adoption, lack of sustainability and low benefits realisation have become the drivers to develop corporate change capability. Leaders of the organisation can no longer only focus on normal day-to-day operations and allow the change team to implement the change. Change capability starts with the top leadership team being effective and proactive leaders of change. Firstly, leaders must '**Articulate** the change vision', secondly, they must '**Model** the new way' and finally, they have to '**Intervene** to ensure sustainable change'.

The **AMI® Model** is based on over thirty years of international change experience and brings together leading practice in change leadership and delivering organisation change. **AMI®** is a comprehensive **Leadership of Change®** model that guides leaders to successfully deliver and achieve organisational change. The model's three critical responsibilities require the leaders who are implementing change to be effective and proactive. Finally, the **AMI® Model** aligns directly with the **a2B Change Management Framework® (a2BCMF®)**, as well as the other **Leadership of Change®** models on sponsorship, behaviour and adoption.

Main Change Leader Responsibilities

The **AMI® Change Leadership Model** outlines the three main responsibilities for effective and proactive change leadership as:

- ➤ **Articulate the Change Vision**: Change leadership is the aptitude to develop and articulate a vision that will inspire the organisation to the new future.

- ➤ **Model the New Way**: The organisation will adopt change when leaders show and model the new way.

- ➤ **Intervene to Ensure Sustainable Change**: Without intervention from leaders, the change will not be adopted or sustained.

2.3 a2B3S® Change Sponsorship Model

a2B3S® Change Sponsorship Model

3 main programme delivery phases | 3 key change sponsorship responsibilities

- Sustain and Close
- Change Definition
- Adoption
- Secure Sponsorship and Resources
- **Sustain**
- **Say**
- Develop New Skills and Behaviours
- Assess Previous Change
- **Support**
- Develop Detailed Change Plan
- Manage Resistance
- Assess Readiness
- Communicate the Change

Sustain · Plan · Execute

a2B3S Change Management Sponsorship

Building the leadership · Enabling Change

a2B Change Management Framework® alignment | Supports change adoption and behaviour change

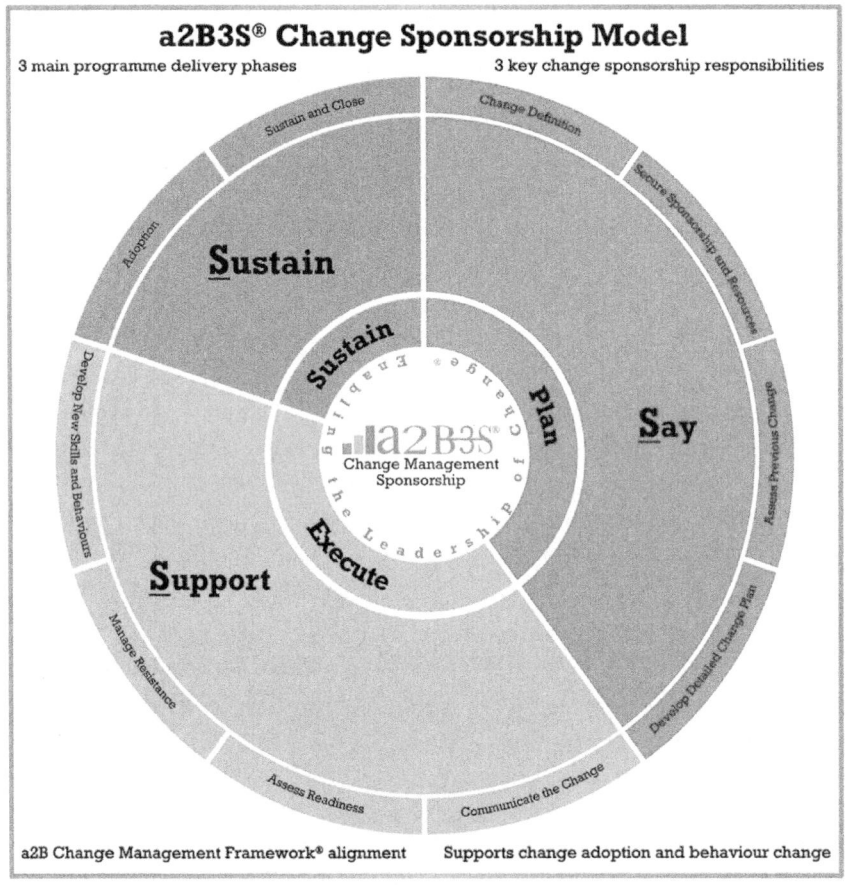

Figure 2.3. a2B3S® Change Sponsorship Model

Without effective and proactive sponsorship the change project will eventually fail, the change will not be adopted by the employees nor be sustained, and it will not deliver the intended benefits

The **a2B3S® Change Sponsorship Model** (**Figure 2.3**) is a structured and disciplined approach for change management sponsors to lead their organisation through a change, the transition from the current 'a' state to the improved future 'B' state. The **a2B3S® Model** has three phases (Plan, Execute and Sustain) which provide change strategies, principles, analysis and tactics to move from one phase to the next. The three critical sponsor responsibilities are: **Say**, **Support** and

Sustain to ensure sustainable change. These responsibilities of the change sponsor are then broken down into sub tasks and activities.

You will rarely encounter a successful change implementation without an effective and proactive sponsor, backed by an aligned leadership team with change leadership skills and knowledge. The successful delivery of the change programme is usually an important element of the organisation's strategy to improve operating performance, be more competitive, etc. These change programmes require finance, organisation resources, time and effort, and the shareholders of the organisation will, at the very least, expect a return on investment (ROI). A sponsor with credibility, influence and authority can play an essential role in delivering the change programme. Part of their role will involve working with the leadership directly to ensure they are actively supporting the change. Other sponsor activities include programme governance, working with the change team and change agents, and intervening with all stakeholders where and when necessary, to reduce resistance.

The **a2B3S® Model** is based on over thirty years of international change experience and brings together leading practice in change sponsorship and delivering organisation change. **a2B3S®** is a comprehensive **Leadership of Change®** model that guides sponsors to successfully deliver and achieve organisational change. The model's three critical responsibilities require the sponsors who are implementing change to be effective and proactive. Finally, the **a2B3S® Model** aligns directly with the **a2B Change Management Framework® (a2BCMF®)**, as well as the other **Leadership of Change®** models on leadership, behaviour and adoption.

Main Change Sponsor Responsibilities

The **a2B3S® Change Sponsorship Model** outlines the three main responsibilities for effective and proactive change sponsorship as:

- ➢ **Say - Communicate the Change**: Articulate the change strategy, be the face of the change and communicate constantly.

- ➢ **Support - Provide Resources, Engage and Coach**: Provide quality resources, engage them, and coach the organisation.

- ➢ **Sustain - Intervene, Reward and Embed**: Intervene to ensure adoption, reward positive behaviour, and embed the new way.

2.4 a2B5R® Employee Behaviour Change Model

a2B5R® Employee Behaviour Change Model
3 main programme delivery phases — 5 steps tailored to suit each client

05 Sustain and Close — Reinforce
01 Change Definition — Recognise
02 Redesign
03 Resolve
04 Replicate

Internal change capability development — Supporting and coaching employees

Figure 2.4 a2B5R® Employee Behaviour Change Model

To solve the employee behaviour problem, the organisation must recognise there is an issue. The new behaviours then need to be redesigned and a resolution made to implement and replicate them. Finally, the new way should be reinforced

One of the most challenging aspects of any change programme is the way in which employee behaviours are addressed. Changing the employee's behaviour and improving their performance is a critical part of the change management process. The **a2B5R® Employee Behaviour Change Model (Figure 2.4)** systematically supports the transition of employee behavioural change from the current 'a' state to the improved future 'B' state.

Behaviours should be considered in the change definition phase and serious thought should be given to this step if change adoption is highly dependent on behavioural change, i.e. it is safety-critical. The initial focus should be on employees with a growth mindset. These employees tend to embrace and be the advocates of change, and they are keen to adopt the new skills and behaviours. They believe that basic skills and behaviours are qualities you can cultivate through your own efforts. Everyone can grow and change through application and experience within the right environment. These employees focus on improving their skills and behaviours to adopt the new change and not on wasting energy by resisting inevitable change. Behaviour change can also be very important when organisations are trying to implement a change that runs counter to its culture. Without a change in employee behaviour and organisation culture, the change may not be successful. A change programme targeting improved customer service is unlikely to be successful if employees treat customers with belligerence, unless it also focuses on employee behaviours.

Developing new behaviours can be a major challenge in adopting and sustaining change. Typically, organisations lose focus and energy towards the end of the change cycle and may not acquire either embedded or lasting change. The **a2B5R® Model** supports the change team to embed the few new behaviours that are critical to change success to achieve the full ROI. Another enabler that should be considered is choice architecture. Choice architecture is the practice of influencing choice by changing the manner in which options are presented to employees.

Five Key Life Cycle Behaviour Change Steps

The **a2B5R® Model** outlines the five steps employees go through in the change transition from the current state 'a' to the improved future state 'B'. The **a2B5R® Model** represents:

- **Recognise**: The first tactic is to officially accept that there is a problem with the current behaviours within the organisation.
- **Redesign**: The second tactic is to agree to define the few new critical behaviours and to redesign a new solution.
- **Resolve**: The third tactic focuses on getting all employees to make a resolution to implement the few new critical behaviours.
- **Replicate**: The fourth tactic is about getting the employee to continue replicating the new behaviours.
- **Reinforce**: The final tactic focuses on ensuring that new behaviours are reinforced so they are embedded.

Section 3: AUILM® Employee Change Adoption Model

Section 3: AUILM® Employee Change Adoption Model

3.0.1 AUILM® Employee Change Adoption Model

AUILM® Employee Change Adoption Model

3 main programme delivery phases — 5 steps tailored to suit each client

- 05 Sustain and Close — Motivation — Adoption — Develop New Skills and Behaviours — 04 Learning — Manage Resistance — Assess Readiness — 03 Involvement — Communicate the Change — Develop Detailed Change Plan — 02 Understanding — Assess Previous Change — Secure Sponsorship and Resources — 01 Change Definition — Awareness

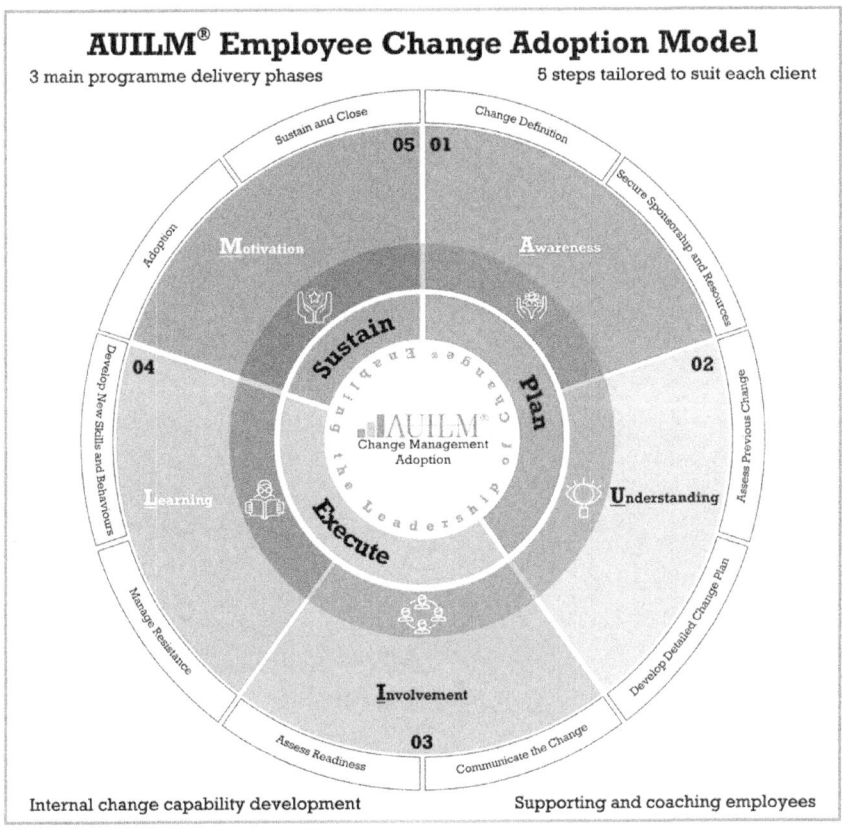

Sustain · Plan · Execute · Enabling Change through Leadership

AUILM® Change Management Adoption

Internal change capability development — Supporting and coaching employees

Figure 3.0.1 AUILM® Employee Change Adoption Model

For change adoption to be successful, support the employees through the change transition by providing awareness, understanding, involvement, learning, and motivation to achieve sustainable change and benefit realisation

Awareness.

Understanding.

Involvement.

Learning.

Motivation.

3.0.2 AUILM® Employee Change Adoption Model - Icons

Awareness: The first tactic is to make the employee aware that there is a new change programme coming, and the change could impact them and their role within the organisation. Awareness should start to happen in the early steps of the change, i.e. when it is announced. Getting the change message out simultaneously, through as many communication channels as possible with a feedback loop for questions, is extremely important.

Understanding: The second tactic is to provide greater insights into the change so that the wider context is understood. This is best done when it is communicated during face-to-face meetings and events. The objective is to create an understanding about why the organisation is making the change and how it will impact employees, as well as what is required from them.

Involvement: The third tactic focuses on involving the employee in the change directly. Analysis from many change history assessments© (CHA©) indicates that employees are never more passionate or stronger than when they have thought up their own arguments for believing what they believe. Keeping employees involved in issues that affect them will reduce resistance and start to gain their buy-in to the change.

Learning: The fourth tactic is about getting the employee to see the change as an opportunity for learning and growth. This step focuses on ensuring the employee has developed the new skills and behaviours for the change to be successful. The employee should be competent in their new role and replicating the new behaviours learnt. The support of the sponsor and the leadership team is still required to reinforce the change.

Motivation: The final tactic focuses on ensuring motivation for sustainable change after the change is passed back to operations and the change team has dissolved. With new skills maturing and the new behaviours being reinforced, the final step is to make sure that employees remain motivated. This will ensure they are positively focused to do their part to improve organisation performance.

3.0.3 AUILM® Model Overview

The **AUILM® Model** (**Figure 3.0.1**) helps teams driving change to understand how employees might react during a change transition, which they may perceive as a threat to them. Although individual employees will react to change differently, the model highlights some emotions each person may feel at different times during the process. It provides a perspective on why there might be resistance, along with solutions the change team could use to counter resistance along the change transition journey. The five key life cycle steps of the **AUILM® Model** support employees as they go through the change transition from the current 'a' state to the improved future 'B' state.

Importance of Employee Change Adoption

Employee change adoption is fundamental to successful organisational change. It is about facilitating and enabling the smooth transition of the organisation and employees from the current state 'a' to the future improved state 'B'. Without full employee adoption of the new technology or new way of working, the organisation is unlikely to improve operating performance, achieve the targeted benefits or return on investment (ROI). The organisation's investment will be lost, as will customers who expect continually improving products and services.

Change adoption is something the change team, leaders and sponsor need to consider well before the start of training or before the change starts to be implemented. It must be a serious consideration at the early stage of change planning (see **a2BCMF© Step 1 - Change Definition**) and the leaders of the organisation need to consider employee change adoption as part of the leadership alignment process (**see Section 3.0.8**). The leaders and sponsor need to ensure the employees are ready and prepared with the new skills and behaviours, with the right motivation to adopt and sustain the change.

Benefits of Employee Change Adoption:

Employees perform their normal day-to-day tasks when suddenly they are hit by change disruption. This is likely to impact their role within the organisation and, more widely, it may even impact their personal lives. Not all employees will embrace the change and everyone will

Section 3: AUILM® Employee Change Adoption Model

react to change differently. The five key steps of the **AUILM® Model** support employees as they go through the change transition, counteracting some of the negative feelings they might be experiencing (**Figure 3.0.3**):

Supporting the Employee Through the Change Adoption Transition

Awareness — Understanding — Involvement — Learning — Motivation

Unsettled — Resentment — Disconnect to Engaged — Competent — Incentivised

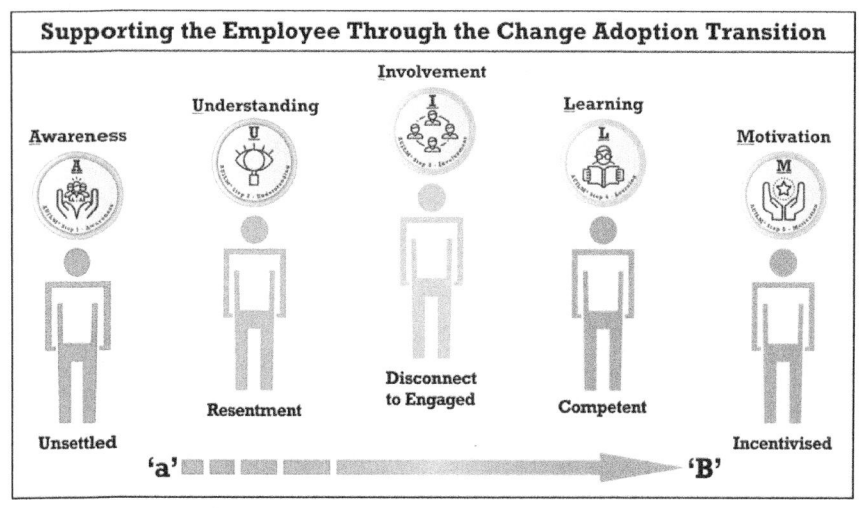

'a' ──────────▶ 'B'

Figure 3.0.3 Employee Change Transition Support

➤ **Awareness**: Counteracts the employee from feeling unsettled.

   o As the employee becomes more aware of the change, they will be less unsettled by it. This should help them avoid or move through the shock and denial stage quickly. Equally, awareness of the change programme helps to stop any disengagement from the organisation or a drop in productivity, etc.

➤ **Understanding**: Counteracts the employee from feeling resentment towards the organisation and the change.

   o As the employee starts to understand the change, they will be less likely to disengage or develop resentment towards it. The aim is to quickly get the employees to understand why the organisation must implement this change, what the changes are to their role and how it will impact them. An employee will worry less when they understand if and how the change will impact them and, ultimately, their families.

➤ **Involvement**: Counteracts the employee from feeling disconnected, moving them towards being engaged with the organisation and the change.

- By involving the employees in the change, there is less chance of them becoming or feeling disconnected from the organisation and the change.
- Over time, the employees become inquisitive and slowly start to become involved in the change. They feel confident that the change will be successful now they will be given the opportunity to develop the skills for their new role and develop the new behaviours. Once they are involved in the change design and have provided input into how they would like the change to be implemented, they want it to work.

➢ **Learning**: Supports the employee to feel competent and ready to operate at the new way of working.

- As the connection to the change builds, the employee discovers an opportunity for learning new skills and behaviours. Being supported to develop the new competencies will equip the employee with the skills, capability and confidence to be a functioning part of the change and the new way of working.

➢ **Motivation**: Supports the employee through incentives, recognising positive performance and adoption.

- An incentive offered through the organisation's reward mechanism acts as the motivation to adopt and sustain the new way of working. The change disruption will soon pass, and the employees should now have the new skills and behaviours that are fast becoming part of normal day-to-day operations.

➢ **Other benefits:**

- **Enhance the Employee's Change Transition Experience**: Employees who are treated well through the change transition will feel valued, motivated and committed to their organisation's change success.
- **Engagement and Collaboration**: Employee engagement and collaboration are primary factors contributing to successful organisations, however both become more important during change implementation.

- **Change Adoption Speed**: Quicker change adoption by the organisation and employees will have a positive impact on how the organisation achieves the targeted benefits and ROI, as well as delivering improved operating performance sooner.

Enablers:

- **Change Management Framework**: Having a programme delivery approach within the Plan, Execute and Sustain phases which considers stakeholder engagement, resistance planning etc.
- **Change Sponsor**: (see 'Sponsor Role' below).
- **Leaders**: Effective and proactive leadership is essential for successful organisational change (**A**rticulate, **M**odel and **I**ntervene).
- **Behaviour Change Focus**: Understanding that employee behaviour change is explicitly linked to successful organisational change.

Barriers:

- **No Change Management Framework**: A communications and training plan are not adequate replacements for a change management framework that drives change programme delivery.
- **No Leadership or Sponsor Support**: Not having effective and proactive leadership and sponsorship throughout the change.
- **No Behaviour Change Focus**: Ignoring the importance of employee behaviour as a change adoption enabler.
- **Bad Change Experience or Fatigue**: Employees who have previously experienced bad change, or too much change, will tend to be more resistant to future change.

Sponsor Role: The importance of having an effective and proactive sponsor in implementing successful change cannot be overstated and will be repeated throughout this book. During all **AUILM®** employee adoption steps, the sponsor's three main responsibilities will be:

- **S**ay: Communicate the change.
- **S**upport: Provide resources, engage and coach.
- **S**ustain: Intervene, reward and embed.

3.0.4 Organisation Change Alignment

Organisational alignment of the employees, its processes and systems, directed by the leadership are critical for change adoption

Organisational alignment can be defined as the extent to which employees, processes and systems are coordinated and focused on a common vision. The leadership team and every employee can then effectively pursue the organisation's strategic objectives. Alignment is the key to any successful organisation during normal day-to-day operations. It is also extremely important when implementing change, especially when there is a focus on either employee change adoption or behaviour change.

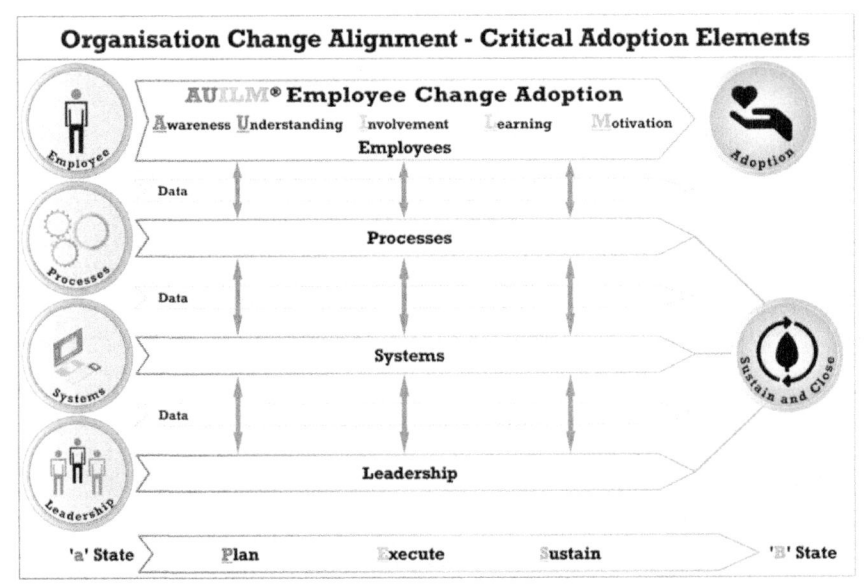

Figure 3.0.4 Change Adoption Organisation Alignment

Organisational change alignment starts with a compelling change vision that inspires employees and gives them purpose. It is supported by the organisation's strategy, values and beliefs. The development of this vision relies on effective and proactive change leadership and as the change vision is articulated by the leaders, then organisational change implementation can commence. Successful change requires the alignment of employees, processes and systems, directed by the leadership (EPSL) and supported by the change team. The key elements that need to be aligned are (**Figure 3.0.4**):

> **Employees**: Individuals hired by an employer to perform a specific role that adds value to the organisation.

> **Processes**: A system of activities by which a business creates a specific result for its customers. These are the foundation of how the organisation operates.

> **Systems**: A set of interconnected devices that provide outputs. They execute and control the internal processes and procedures that deliver the organisation's products or services.

> **Leadership**: Individuals leading the organisation who are collectively responsible for strategy execution and its inherent change programmes.

These four elements will be needed to transition the organisation from the current '**a**' state at the start of the change through to the future '**B**' state. Change implementation will be successful when the employees adopt the change and when the organisation can sustain and close the change programme. Some of the practical benefits of achieving organisation change alignment are:

> Increased speed of change implementation.

> Improved employee engagement and higher adoption rates.

> More effective use of organisational resources.

> Increased leadership credibility and respect.

> Increased customer satisfaction through higher quality products and services.

The rest of this section provides more detail on these four key elements (EPSL):

A. **Employees**.

B. **Processes**.

C. **Systems**.

D. **Leadership**.

3.0.5 Employee Support and Alignment

If the employees are to adopt the change, they need to be supported by the leadership, so they are able to operate within the new way of working, using the organisation's processes and systems

An employee is an individual who was hired by an employer to perform a specific role that adds value to the organisation. The right employees are an organisation's key asset and offer core competitive advantage. Treat employees well and develop them so they can achieve success, and with the right strategy and leadership an organisation can become a global leader. Employees who are supported and aligned with the change bring numerous advantages for the organisation, and very few organisational changes (if any) will be successful without them. To realise these advantages and achieve successful change, employees need the following:

➢ **Employee Change Life Cycle Support**: The employee needs support through the change transition to achieve full adoption:

  o **Awareness**: Making the employee aware that there is a new change programme coming.

  o **Understanding**: Continuing employee engagement to help them understand the business case for change.

  o **Involvement**: Including the employee in the change design to shape the change and gain buy-in.

  o **Learning**: Developing the employee's new skills and behaviours so they can adopt the change.

  o **Motivation**: Creating an employee reward mechanism to motivate employees and reinforce organisational change.

- > **Process Competence**: The employee needs to be trained and have follow-up coaching so they can operate and follow the latest process in the new way of working.

- > **System Competence**: The employee needs to be trained and have follow-up coaching so they can operate the new systems which can, in some cases, be much more complex to operate than the previous ones. Being ready and able for the 'go live' dates can add further challenges.

- > **Leadership**: The employee needs to experience effective and proactive leadership throughout the change with no 'say do' gaps. Leaders need to:
  - **Articulate** the change vision.
  - **Model** the new way.
  - **Intervene** to ensure sustainable change.

Individual employees will react to change differently, some will worry about their capability, job security, future role or ultimately how the change could impact their families. The current 'a' state can have tremendous holding power, and the uncertainty of the future '**B**' state can create resistance. Engaging, supporting and aligning employees with the change will massively encourage successful organisation change implementation. The main goal for the organisation is to have the right employees with the rights skills to operate the new processes and systems proficiently. There are also shared benefits for both the organisation and the employees if they are supported through the change transition process and aligned with the other key change elements (EPSL). These are:

- > Enhanced employee change experience.
- > Improved employee engagement and collaboration.
- > Reduced stress and anxiety about the change.
- > Reduced employee change resistance.
- > Improved change design solution quality and acceptance.
- > Increased speed of change implementation.
- > Higher user adoption rates and successful sustainable change.

3.0.6 Process Alignment

At the core of any successful organisation there are aligned business processes, operated by competent employees using effective business systems

Business processes can be defined as a set of activities by which an organisation creates a specific result for its customers. They are the foundation of how the organisation operates, adds customer value and how it achieves its objectives. An organisation that can successfully align the new processes with the rest of the organisation should have improved operating performance. The interrelationships and interdependencies between employees, processes and systems must be understood. The change implementation will not be successful if these elements are not aligned and operating proficiently together.

To successfully implement the change, the new processes need to be aligned with employees and the organisation's systems. The following activities need to be executed:

> **Employee Process Competency**: Unless the employees fully understand and can operate the new processes, the new way of working will not happen, and the change will not be implemented.
>
> o **Training and Coaching**: Process training comprises a series of steps that need to be followed systematically to enable an efficient training programme. This systematic approach to training ensures that employees are prepared for their new work by having the necessary knowledge, skills, and behaviours to operate the new processes.
>
> o **Process Understanding**: Process improvement professionals would argue that most employees lack fundamental process understanding. Having an understanding of the process in

terms of suppliers, inputs, process steps, outputs and customers (SIPOC) supports consistent replication to meet customer specifications.

- **Processes**: At the very least, an employee needs the standard operating procedures (SOPs) to execute a process. However, these are only high-level and usually only describe the 'who', 'what' and 'when'. The standard work instructions (SWI) provide more detail and include step by step, detailed task level instructions.

- **Systems**: As part of the system operating manual (SOM) documentation (or equivalent), there should be a clear reference to how the system operates in conjunction with the new processes.

- **Leadership**: The leaders of the organisation should ensure the newly defined processes have every chance of being executed to deliver the specified products or services as per the customers' requirements. The leaders should be involved in the process design, delivery and subsequent appraisal to develop the employee's new skills and knowledge. They should also ensure there is:
  - Effective training, supported with follow-up coaching.
  - Documented operator process instructions, job aids, etc.
  - Operator personal protective equipment (PPE), tools, aids, etc.
  - Product or service quality acceptance criteria.

If the proper processes are not in place and working effectively, they will probably fail, no matter how good the systems are. The main benefits of the organisation having effective and proficient processes that support successful change implementation are:

- Less stressful employee working environment.
- Consistent replication and standards of product and service quality, enabling customer satisfaction and loyalty.
- Well designed and successfully implemented business processes can increase competitive advantage.
- Well defined and documented processes create a baseline for improvement.

3.0.7 Systems Alignment

Implementing a new business system without employee, process and leadership alignment will likely cause organisation chaos and lower operating performance

A system can be defined as a set of interconnected devices that provide outputs. Business systems are important because they provide an organisation with a framework within which to operate and this can have a dramatic effect on efficiency and productivity. Systems execute and control the internal processes and procedures that deliver the organisation's products or services. If the proper systems are not in place and working effectively, no matter how good the supporting processes are, they will probably fail. Organisations that can successfully implement business systems into the organisation should demonstrate improved operating performance. The interrelationships and interdependencies between employees, processes and systems must be understood. The change implementation will not be successful if these elements operate in isolation.

To successfully implement the change, the new systems need to be aligned with employees and processes. The following activities need to be executed:

> ➢ **Employee System Competency**: If the change team does not plan for how the employees will operate and interact with new systems, then adoption of the new ways of working will be limited. The employees need to be equipped with the right skills, knowledge and tools to operate the new systems. This might also include behaviour training to ensure system compliance and prevent system circumvention issues.

> ➢ **Processes**: The organisation's processes must be aligned with the new systems as they cannot operate in isolation. The change team

should ensure both the process and systems team work together with multiple stage-gate reviews to ensure that the processes and systems are compatible and synchronised.

- ➢ **Systems**: Most large organisations would be unable to operate without business systems. New systems tend to be more complex, perform more activities for an organisation and, in most cases, need more capable and talented employees to operate them. This usually means providing timely training and detailed high quality system end user manuals, followed up with coaching from systems superusers to close any competency gaps.

- ➢ **Leadership**: The leaders of the organisation should ensure the installed business systems have every chance of being executed to deliver the specified products or services as per the customers' requirements. The leaders should be involved in the design, delivery and subsequent appraisal to develop the employee's new skills and knowledge. They should also ensure there is effective training, supported by follow-up coaching and the employee has the appropriate system end user manuals, etc.

There are important benefits for the organisation if the new systems are implemented as per their design specification and they are operated fully by the employees. If properly implemented, the right business systems benefit the organisation in terms of:

- ➢ **Consistency**: Good business systems bring consistency to an organisation's business activities. They ensure that all employees perform their activities the same way each time.

- ➢ **Operational Efficiency**: Business systems can automate back-office functions as well as repetitive tasks, thus reducing staff numbers and costs.

- ➢ **Scalability**: Business systems can be the building blocks to grow an organisation. Developing replicable, scalable business systems will enable the organisation to take on more customers, etc.

- ➢ **Data Management**: Improved data accuracy can help improve business processes and decision-making.

3.0.8 Leadership Alignment

*The change leader has three key responsibilities for the successful leadership of change, they are **A**rticulate, **M**odel and **I**ntervene*

The leaders of the organisation are collectively responsible for strategy execution and its inherent change programmes. Change leadership is about being a proactive growth mindset leader or employee who has the knowledge, skills and ability to successfully transition an organisation from the current state 'a' to the future state 'B', ensuring adoption and benefits realisation. This transition involves planning and executing the change so that the organisation and its employees can sustain the change or transformation. The change leader has three key responsibilities for the successful leadership of change, they are **A**rticulate, **M**odel and **I**ntervene.

The leaders of the organisation play a critical role in organisation change, they must be effective and proactive throughout change implementation. To achieve successful organisational change, leaders should ensure their employees are prepared and aligned with the new processes and systems, this involves:

> **Employee Collaboration and Involvement**: The leaders must create a shared change vision through communication, engagement and persuasion that touches feelings and emotions to enlist employee and organisation support. Employees should participate in the change design, as those who are involved will find it difficult to reject its implementation. Leaders must model the new skills and behaviours and then support their employees to learn them. They should also offer a little nudge or intervene directly to ensure full employee adoption.

Section 3: AUILM® Employee Change Adoption Model

- **Process Implementation Involvement**: Leaders need to ensure the news processes are fully implemented and aligned with the new systems. For this to be successful, the leaders need to be involved in process design and give their final stamp of approval. The employees need to be trained and coached to develop the new competencies to operate the new processes. If leaders adopt a superficial approach to this task, the planned and budgeted training may not provide the employees with the required process skills and knowledge.

- **System Implementation Involvement**: Leaders need to ensure the new systems are fully implemented and aligned with the new processes. Similar to their involvement in process implementation, the leaders need to be involved in the selection, design and approval of the new systems. They must ensure that training budgets are protected and that the change readiness assessment (CRA) indicates their employees are competent and ready for the agreed 'go live' dates.

- **Leadership**: Effective and proactive leadership throughout the change implementation requires the change leaders to:
  - **Articulate** the change vision.
  - **Model** the new way.
  - **Intervene** to ensure sustainable change.

The main benefits of the organisation having effective and proactive change leadership are:

- Reduced change resistance through employee involvement.
  - Improved change design solution, quality and acceptance.
  - Reduced employee stress and anxiety through the change.
  - Improved employee engagement and collaboration.
- Higher user adoption rates and successful sustainable change.
- Increased speed of change implementation, meeting programme schedule dates and milestones.
- Return on investment (ROI) and full benefits realisation is achieved, along with improved business performance.

Section 3.1: <u>A</u>wareness - Plan Phase

3.1 AUILM® - Awareness

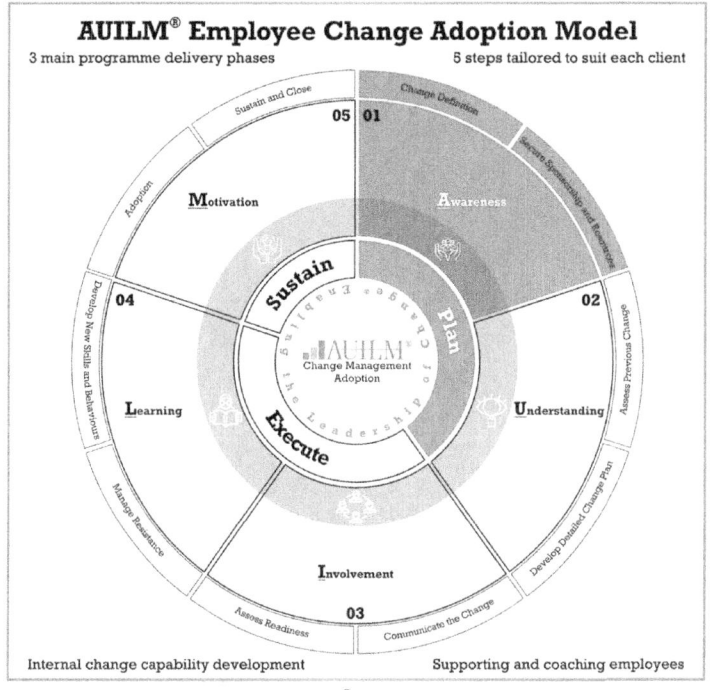

Figure 3.1 AUILM® Model - Awareness

Plan: Setting the change programme up for success.

Section 3.1 Awareness - Structure

3.1.0 AUILM®: Awareness Overview.

3.1.1 Employee: What's In It For Me (WIIFM)?

3.1.2 Processes: Creating Process Change Awareness.

3.1.3 Systems: Creating System Change Awareness.

3.1.4 Leadership: Creating Change Vision Awareness

3.1.5 a2BCMF® Step 1.1. Change Capacity.

3.1.6 a2BCMF® Step 1.2: Change Elevator Speech.

3.1.7 a2BCMF® Step 2.1: Sponsorship.

3.1.8 a2BCMF® Step 2.2: Change Agents.

3.1.9 a2BCMF® Figure: Steps 1 - 2.

3.1.10 a2BCMF® Table: Steps 1 - 2.

3.1.0 AUILM®: Awareness Overview

Creating employee change awareness must start on day one, otherwise information gaps will cause fear, resistance will start to build and this will hinder adoption

Awareness: The first tactic is to make the employee aware that there is a new change programme coming and the change could impact them and their role within the organisation. **Awareness** should start to happen in the early stages of the change, i.e. when it is announced. Getting the change message out is extremely important. This should be done using as many communication channels as possible and have a feedback loop for questions. Gaps in any change communication will quickly be filled by rumours and resistance. Creating employee change awareness is typically about clarifying:

- **What**: What the change programme is about:
    - Improving products, services, etc.
    - Meeting changing customer expectations, etc.
- **Why**: Why this change programme is so important to the organisation:
    - The need to better compete against competitors.
    - New technology is changing the way the organisation operates.
- **Benefits**: What the advantages are if this change is implemented successfully. Benefits can be both tangible and intangible.
- **What's In It For Me? (WIIFM)**: This is the foremost question that employees are concerned with when hearing about organisational change. Starting to be aware of WIIFM helps the

employee rationalise how the change could impact them and their families, and how they will respond to it.

Importance of Employee Change Awareness

Early consideration of employee change adoption is extremely important and must start on day one. Change adoption starts with change awareness and making the employees and the organisation aware of the change should start as soon as possible. There is a tendency in some organisations not to share the details about the change programme early. For example, there may be a perception that employees can be ignored until implementation and therefore the leadership team might think they can delay communication about the change until it is almost ready to be launched or the training starts. Consequently, the benefits of gradually bringing employees on board and taking them through the change transition could be overlooked.

Benefits of Creating Employee Awareness:

- **Starting Employee, Processes, Systems and Leadership Alignment**: Successful change requires the alignment of these four elements, supported by the change team.
- **Prevents Resistance**: Early change awareness helps to prevent employee resistance from developing which can negatively impact implementation speed and limit benefit realisation.
- **Builds a Strong Change Foundation**: If the employee is made aware of the change on day one, in a clear way, the change starts on a strong positive foundation.
- **Builds Trust**: By making employees aware of the change early, the organisation and the leaders start to build trust with them and any impacted stakeholders. This trust is fundamental as the employee moves through the **AUILM®** cycle of **Awareness**, **Understanding**, **Involvement**, **Learning** and **Motivation** to ensure sustainable change.

Enablers:

- Effective and proactive change sponsorship (**Say**).

- ➤ Preparing to align employees, processes, systems and the leadership.
- ➤ Effective and proactive change leadership (**Articulate**).
- ➤ Using the **a2B Change Management Framework®** to guide the change programme through **Step 1 - Change Definition** and **Step 2 - Secure Sponsorship and Resources**.
- ➤ The sponsor aligning the leadership team and guiding them to develop a compelling change vision that is aligned to the organisation's strategy, values and beliefs to inspire employees with purpose.
- ➤ Constantly communicating a clear and concise change message (what, why, benefits and WIIFM) with a feedback loop.
- ➤ Stressing the importance of aligning employees with the new processes and systems, supported by the organisational leaders.
- ➤ Other enablers:
  - o Communicating a detailed change roadmap with stakeholders.
  - o Communicating a strong and detailed business case for change.
  - o Growth mindset employees.
  - o Performing stakeholder identification, analysis and mapping.
  - o Preparing for employee resistance.

Barriers:

- ➤ No change sponsor or one who is not effective and proactive when nominated.
- ➤ Not preparing to align employees, processes, systems and the leadership.
- ➤ No leadership support or a leadership team who are not effective and proactive change leaders.
- ➤ Not using a change management framework or equivalent to guide the change programme on critical elements, such as defining the change and securing sponsorship.

3.1 AUILM® - Awareness

- Thinking that achieving employee adoption is a singular process to implement successful sustainable change.
- The leaders not having a change vision or articulating one that is not realistic and does not appeal to the employee's hearts and minds.
- Launching the change programme without effective communication, which allows rumours or misinformation to fill the communication vacuum.
- Leaders thinking that a one-off change communication 'WIIFM' message will win over impacted stakeholders.
- Competing for resources against other initiatives without having quantified benefits.
- Other barriers:
  - No roadmap with the high-level change deliverables that can be used to communicate with stakeholders.
  - Change fatigue or limited change capacity.
  - Implementing a change into an organisation that runs counter to its culture.
  - A weak business case for change.
  - Thinking there will be no resistance.
  - Thinking that stakeholder identification, analysis and mapping is an unnecessary luxury.

Sponsor Role: During the **AUILM® Awareness** and **Understanding** employee adoption steps, the sponsor's main responsibility and sub activities will be:

Say - Communicate the Change:

- Articulate the change strategy.
- Be the face of the change.
- Communicate constantly.

3.1.1 Employee: What's In It For Me (WIIFM)?

One of the first things an employee asks themselves when they hear about organisation change is 'What's in it for me?'

When an employee first hears about change, the first thing they think of is 'What's In It For Me' (WIIFM)? Answering this through as many communication channels as possible, with a feedback loop for questions, is extremely important. Gaps in any change communication will quickly be filled by rumours and resistance. Change **Awareness** is about being transparent, answering any concerns about the change. This should help to address any emotional, financial, job security or competency fears an employee may have. **Awareness** answers the basic questions we all have when change is introduced:

➢ **Why is it changing?**
  o Why is there a business need?
  o What is the business case?
  o What is the vision for change? (**see Section 3.1.4**)
  o What is the risk of not changing?

The change team should have crafted a tailored answer for each of the above questions when engaging and communicating with stakeholders (**a2BCMF® Step 5 - Communicate the Change**). The objective is to make sure that the employees gain awareness of the change with messages that will resonate with them. The change message should focus on employee benefits from the change, as well as reduce any fears they may have regarding job security, training, etc. The importance of the organisation's leaders and the sponsor articulating the change vision cannot be overstated.

3.1.2 Processes: Creating Process Change Awareness

I know these processes and there is nothing wrong with them. This is more change for the sake of change

Organisational change often impacts existing processes, they may be modified, replaced or made obsolete. This will impact both the employees who operate the existing processes and the organisation which needs solid processes to perform effectively to deliver its products and services.

There will be employee concerns when they hear that processes will change from the ones they know and operate. Employees may have anxieties about how they will gain the new skills and knowledge to operate the new or adjusted processes, or they may worry that they will not be needed when the new processes start. It is imperative that the change team and leaders quickly engage the impacted employees and address these concerns. The change team should also work with the function or department responsible for the organisation's processes. The employees need to be reassured that they will be given support throughout the change journey. This should include:

- ➤ New standard work instructions (SWI) or equivalent.
- ➤ New operator process training and follow-up coaching.
- ➤ Workload considerations during the transition period.

If the organisation makes the employee aware of how they will be supported to operate the new processes, then their concerns should be minimised. They will start to trust the organisation and be more confident in the change transition. However, done badly, the opposite can happen, and a lack of trust and change resistance will grow.

3.1.3 Systems: Creating System Change Awareness

Our systems are fine. New technology could make things worse

Systems are essential building blocks of nearly every organisation, they connect all of an organisation's intricate parts and help it achieve its goals. Advancements in technology means that systems are continually improving, and organisations need to keep updating them. Systems can be a major financial investment, requiring rigorous planning, many resources and a lot of effort to make them successful.

The mention of introducing new business systems can make some employees feel nervous. Some will remember the last major system introduction with trepidation and may even despair when thinking about repeating a similar experience. Employees may also be concerned about learning the new system. Changes and updates to systems often involve more complexity and require higher levels of system access, meaning that those who use it need to be more senior. In some cases, systems can be less complex, and the user's role could change or even become obsolete. Either way, this is a challenge that the change team have to deal with, likely involving some early and difficult discussions.

The change team need to work closely with the system vendor to fully understand resourcing and skills requirements. The employees then need to be reassured that they will be given support and appropriate resources to develop the system skills and knowledge. This should be clearly defined, well communicated and include:

- ➤ New system operating manual (SOM) or equivalent.
- ➤ New operator system training onsite or with the vendor.
- ➤ Follow-up coaching by a superuser to close identified gaps.

3.1.4 Leadership: Creating Change Vision Awareness

Most successful change implementations have an effective and proactive sponsor backed by an aligned leadership team with change leadership skills and knowledge

Successful delivery of organisational change cannot be achieved without the full support of the organisation's leaders. They must be effectively and proactively involved throughout all five critical **AUILM®** steps of the change implementation. The leader's first responsibility is to help create **AUILM® Awareness**.

In order to prepare for organisational change implementation, leaders will have completed the leadership alignment process, and their first responsibility as the change management leadership team is to '**Articulate** the change vision'. Change leadership is all about having a vision of what the organisation will look like when it moves from the current '**a**' state to the improved future '**B**' state. This change vision must succinctly describe how the organisation, product or service will look after the change is successfully implemented in the time limit specified. It should be bold but realistic and it should paint a vivid picture of the future state that appeals to the employee's hearts and minds. The change vision should be carefully crafted with the involvement of the leadership team as they will be the main communicators of this vision. The vision must be communicated consistently and often, to start creating employee change awareness.

A significant challenge for all change professionals when implementing organisation change is working with a leader who only focuses on normal day-to-day operations and ignores change activities. The change team and sponsor should intervene to prevent this from happening as it will negatively impact change implementation.

3.1.5 a2BCMF® Step 1.1 Change Capacity

Organisation change capacity and employee workload are ignored in change implementation, until they become the reason for failure

Estimated Organisation Capacity for Change

- Normal Day-to-Day Operations: 85%
- Unplanned Work or Rework: 7%
- Mandatory Change Capacity: 2%
- Strategic Change Capacity: 6%

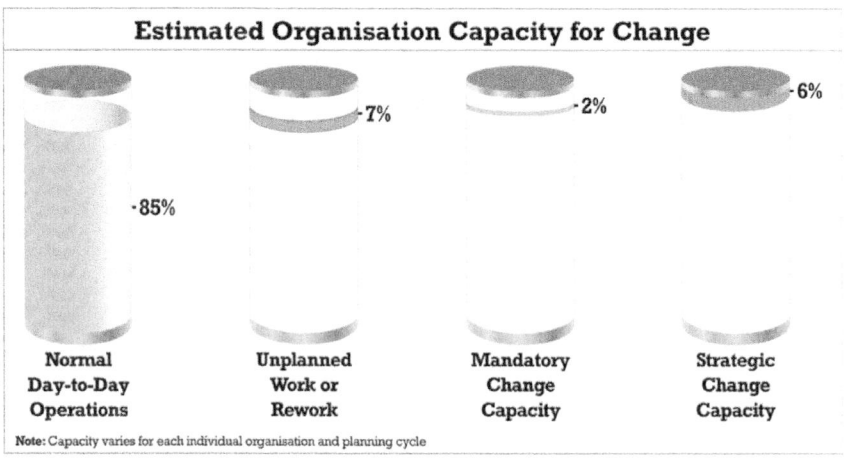

Note: Capacity varies for each individual organisation and planning cycle

Figure 3.1.5 Estimated Organisation Capacity for Change

An organisation only has so much capacity for change while normal day-to-day operations continue. Pushing too much change into the organisation at the same time will limit successful implementation. It could also put extra workload pressures on the employees who may then resist the change or be unable to adopt the new way of working.

An organisation's strategic planning process should outline the required resources and how much capacity is needed. The remaining capacity should be an important consideration for change sponsors and their teams when planning their change programmes. There are typically four key organisational capacity components:

> **Normal Day-to-Day Operations**: The activities that a business and its employees engage in on a daily basis for the purposes of generating a profit.

> **Unplanned Work or Rework**: Additional, unplanned or corrective non-conformance work that enters the organisation.

> **Mandatory Change Capacity**: Financial, legal, health and safety requirements, etc that must be implemented.

> **Strategic Change Capacity**: Optional change the organisation can select to do.

3.1.6 a2BCMF® Step 1.2 Change Elevator Speech

Effective change communication is about getting the right message to the right stakeholders at the right time, in their frame of reference with a feedback loop

Change Elevator Speech

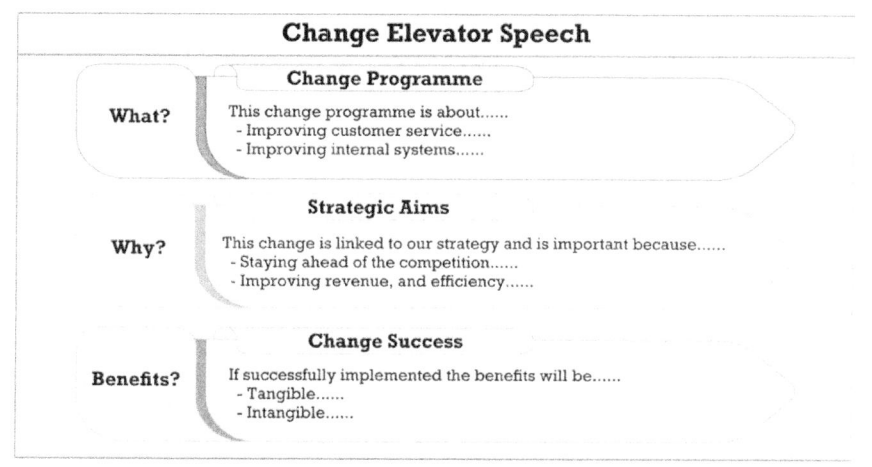

What?	**Change Programme**	This change programme is about...... - Improving customer service...... - Improving internal systems......
Why?	**Strategic Aims**	This change is linked to our strategy and is important because...... - Staying ahead of the competition...... - Improving revenue, and efficiency......
Benefits?	**Change Success**	If successfully implemented the benefits will be...... - Tangible...... - Intangible......

Figure 3.1.6 Change Elevator Speech

A well-constructed change elevator speech will help to communicate the change to gain stakeholder support and buy-in, as well as help to sell the change case to secure critical organisation resources. It can help to communicate the most important aspects of the change programme within a short amount of time. It can also be used as part of all stakeholder communications, helping to communicate a consistent change message. If done well and early, it can help to prevent rumours from starting and resistance from building.

The change elevator speech should be a clear, concise business message, the 'commercial' or 'advertisement' of the change programme. It communicates the 'What', 'Why' and the 'Benefits' of the change programme. The elevator speech should be no longer than eighty to a hundred words or eight to ten sentences.

The process of developing the change elevator speech should follow a properly facilitated and structured approach as it usually takes several sessions to develop a succinct and memorable message. It should be practiced and tested before conveying it to the wider stakeholder community. It should also be aligned with the leadership's first responsibility, '**Articulate** the change vision'. The importance and the impact of the change elevator speech cannot be overstated.

3.1.7 a2BCMF® Step 2.1 Sponsorship

Without effective and proactive sponsorship the change programme will eventually fail, the change will not be adopted by the employees or sustained, and it will not deliver the intended benefits

Key Elements of Successful Sponsorship

- Intervene to ensure adoption
- Reward good behaviour
- Embed and adopt the new way

Sustain

Say
- Articulate the strategy
- The face of the project
- Communicate constantly

- Provide quality resources
- Engage the organisation
- Coach the organisation

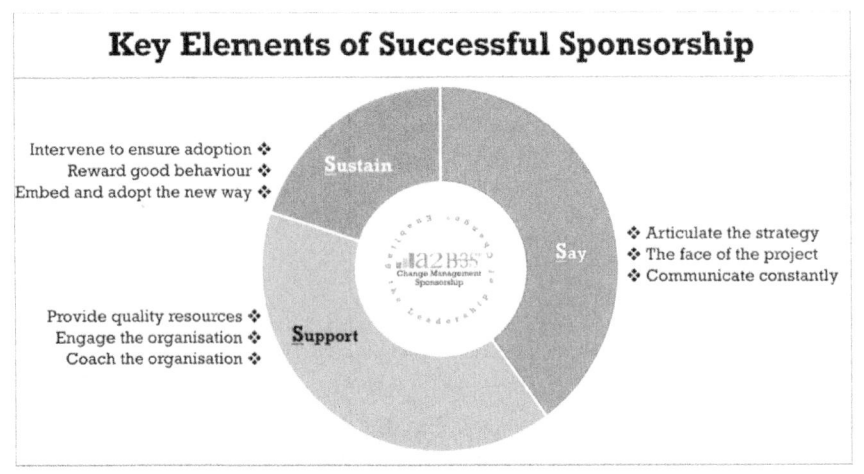

Support

Figure 3.1.7 Key Elements of Sponsorship

The identification of the appropriate change sponsor should be one of the first tasks within any change programme, and it should happen as soon as possible after the 'Change Definition' is completed. Delivery of the change programme is a strategic element of the organisation's portfolio and a capital investment in terms of organisation resources, time and effort. This investment should provide a return to the organisation through improved financial performance.

A sponsor's role is to be personally involved in leading and owning the change, this involves the three main responsibilities: **Say**, **Support**, and **Sustain**. The sponsor is primarily concerned with ensuring that the change programme delivers the agreed upon business benefits. They play a vital leadership role and the bigger the change programme, the more senior the sponsor should be. The sponsor is usually a trusted senior executive with many years of experience and with widely accepted organisational creditability.

Without effective and proactive sponsorship the change programme will eventually fail, the change will not be adopted nor sustained, and it will not deliver the intended benefits. Getting the right person and character to be the sponsor is extremely important.

3.1.8 a2BCMF® Step 2.2 Change Agents

Change agents with organisation credibility, change management skills and the desire to improve an organisation can greatly enhance change adoption

Change Agents - Internal Versus External

Internal Change Agents

Advantages:
- Can be released to the programme immediately and be ready to start

Disadvantages:
- Will not usually have change management skills, tools or a framework to use

External Change Agents (Consultants)

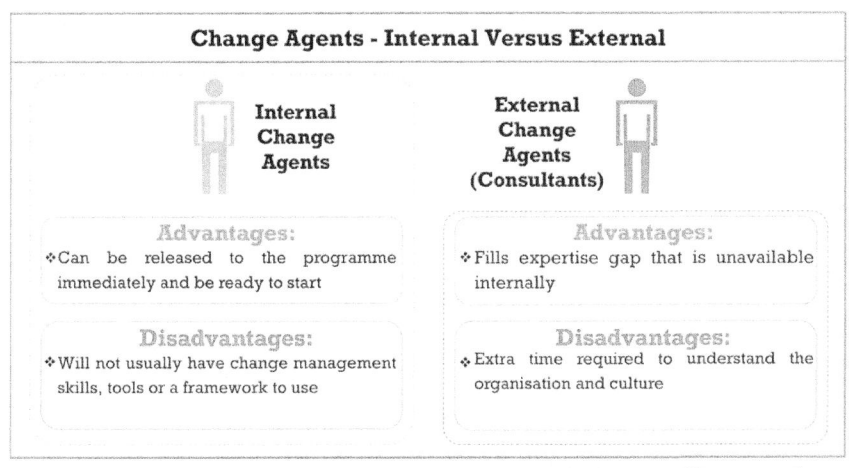

Advantages:
- Fills expertise gap that is unavailable internally

Disadvantages:
- Extra time required to understand the organisation and culture

Figure 3.1.8 Change Agents - Internal Versus External

Change agents can be an organised group, leaders or individuals that undertake the task of leading, communicating and facilitating change in an organisation. They are the nominated advocates for change and can be internal or external to the organisation. Both types of change agents have advantages and disadvantages.

Change agents can make an invaluable contribution to the organisation's change, especially if the change is being implemented across the organisation. They can play a vital role in supporting the leadership team, helping to sell their vision, as well as being their eyes and ears in the workplace. Change agents with organisation credibility and change skills can be the leader's business change partner, providing a conduit to the employees to enhance change adoption.

The success of any change effort depends heavily on the relationship between the change agent, the change team, the sponsor, the leadership team and the employees of the organisation. To be successful, change agents develop relationships built on trust and commitment, they are genuinely interested in other people and the impacted stakeholders. They should have credibility within the organisation, both in terms of their knowledge and their character.

3.1.9 a2B Change Management Framework® Steps 1 - 2

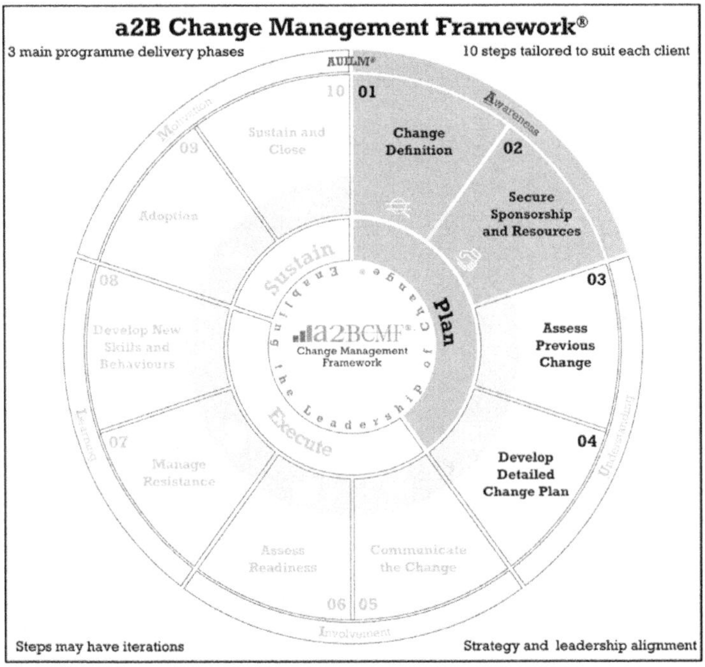

Figure 3.1.9 Change Management Framework® Steps 1 - 2

Adhering to **a2BCMF® Steps 1 and 2** can enhance employee change adoption and implementation success in the following ways:

> **Change Definition**: Unless the change programme is continually aligned to the organisation's strategy and capacity it will not deliver speedy benefits or value to the organisation. There is little value focusing on employee change adoption if the change programme will not improve organisation performance.

> **Secure Sponsorship and Resources**: Without effective and proactive sponsorship, the change programme will eventually fail, the change will not be adopted by the employees or sustained, and it will not deliver the intended benefits. A sponsor with organisation credibility, seniority and time to perform the role can ensure the leaders release competent resources to the change team, provide oversight, ensure timely decisions, approve deliverables, etc.

3.1 AUILM® - Awareness

Each of the **AUILM®** sections will list essential **a2BCMF®** change concepts. However, there are other concepts that can be important to an organisation, depending on their change. **Table 3.1.10** below outlines some selected change concepts leaders of change should consider during the Plan phase (see **Change Management Handbook - Leadership of Change® Volume 3**).

a2B Change Management Framework® (a2BCMF®) Considerations
Step 1 - Change Definition
Business Case: Developed to assess the change programme's balance between costs and benefits. It also serves as a formal declaration of the value that the programme is expected to deliver and a justification for the resources that will be expended to deliver it.
Change Roadmap: A graphical time order representation of the programme's intended direction and a set of documented success criteria for each of the scheduled events. The roadmap will help to quickly communicate the high-level change plan, benefits and goals.
Benefits Plan and Tracker: Used for the identification, definition, planning, tracking and realisation of business benefits through the Plan, Execute and Sustain phases of the change programme.
Stakeholder Mapping: The visual representation of stakeholder analysis. It organises impacted stakeholders according to the key criteria defined in the earlier analysis. Stakeholder mapping is essential for the success of a change programme and will help in better managing potential resistance and expectations.
Governance: The systems and methods of how the change programme will be authorised, monitored and supported by its sponsoring organisation. Programme governance refers to the structure, practices and processes which ensure that change programmes are managed throughout their life cycle.
Step 2 - Secure Sponsorship and Resources
Core Change Team Resources: If the change programme is important to the organisation's strategy and future success, a dedicated change team may be needed. This team will help the leaders define the change management strategy, tools, plans and then support implementation.
Change Agents: An organised group, leaders or individuals that undertake the task of leading, communicating and facilitating change in an organisation.

Table 3.1.10 Step 1 - 2 a2BCMF® Change Considerations

Section 3.2: <u>U</u>nderstanding - Plan Phase

3.2 A<u>U</u>ILM® - <u>U</u>nderstanding

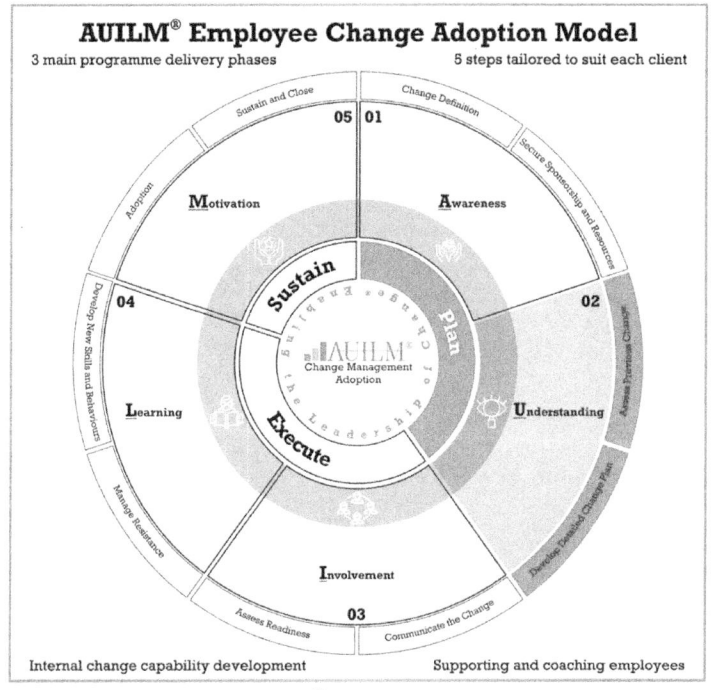

Figure 3.2 A<u>U</u>ILM® Model - <u>U</u>nderstanding

Plan: Setting the change programme up for success.

Section 3.2 <u>U</u>nderstanding - Structure

3.2.0 A<u>U</u>ILM®: <u>U</u>nderstanding Overview.

3.2.1 Employee: How Will this Change Impact Me?

3.2.2 Processes: Understand Why Processes Change.

3.2.3 Systems: Understand Why Systems Change.

3.2.4 Leadership: Creating Change Vision Understanding.

3.2.5 a2BCMF® Step 3.1: Organisation Structure.

3.2.6 a2BCMF® Step 3.2: Organisation Workload.

3.2.7 a2BCMF® Step 4.1: Learning Plan.

3.2.8 a2BCMF® Step 4.2: Resistance Strategy Plan (RSP).

3.2.9 a2BCMF® Figure: Steps 3 - 4.

3.2.10 a2BCMF® Table: Steps 3 - 4.

3.2.0 AUILM®: Understanding Overview

An early major change adoption challenge for the organisation is making sure the employee understands the business reason for change, as well as how it impacts them

Understanding: The second tactic is to provide greater insights into the change so that the wider context is understood. This is best done when communicated face-to-face at meetings and events. The objective is to create an **Understanding** about why the organisation is making the change and how it will impact employees, as well as what is required from them. Building on an employee's awareness of the change and explaining exactly what is going to change and how it will impact them, helps employees to understand and starts to prepare them for change involvement:

> **Understanding the Overall Change to the Organisation**: Employees will gain an understanding of the business case study and how it fits with the organisation's strategy.

  o Cost benefit analysis, alternative solutions, the risk of not changing and business and operational impacts.

> **Change Impact to the Employee**: How the change will impact the way the employee works, their role, job description, department etc. This will include an understanding of:

  o Changes to existing processes.

  o Changes to existing systems.

  o Support from the organisation's leaders.

Importance of Employee Change Understanding

Understanding builds on the **Awareness** step when the employee is first introduced to the change. The leadership should explain the external forces that have caused the organisation to change from the old way of operating and why it is necessary to implement the change. When the leadership articulates the change vision, supported by the sponsor articulating the change strategy, the business case for the change should become clear. This should help to demonstrate the negative consequences for the organisation if it does not implement the change. As the employee starts to understand the change, they will be less likely to disengage, resent it or develop resistance towards it.

The aim is to get the employee to see the positive WIIFM and the benefits to the organisation. As the employee understands the need for change and the impact to them, they will be more likely to engage and get involved in shaping the change. Employee engagement and involvement will enhance the change design, adoption rates and change implementation speed. Likewise, the opposite may happen if the leadership team and sponsor fail to get the employees to understand the business reason for change. However, some changes may have negative implications for employees and a strategy should be planned to deal with this emotive issue.

Benefits of Creating Employee Understanding:

- **Foundation for Engagement and Preparation for Involvement**: The engaged employee is more likely to get involved and provide input into the change design.

- **Developing Trust**: Leaders having honest business discussions and showing the employee empathy will go a long way towards developing trust, which will be needed throughout the **AUILM**® cycle.

- **Enhance the Employee Change Experience**: The leaders of change play a critical role by engaging the employee through the change **AUILM**® cycle, this can either enhance the experience or provoke resistance. Treat the employees well so they feel valued, motivated, committed to their organisation's goals and values and contribute to organisational change success.

Enablers:

- Continued effective and proactive change sponsorship (**Say**).
- Starting to align employees, processes, systems and the leadership.
- Continued effective and proactive change leadership (**Articulate**).
- Using the **a2B Change Management Framework®** to guide the change programme through **Step 3 - Assess Previous Change** and **Step 4 - Develop Detailed Change Plan**.
- Leadership articulating an inspiring change vision that resonates with employees, to enlist employee and organisation support.
- Communicating how the employees will be aligned with the new processes and systems, supported by the organisational leaders.
- Performing the change history assessment© (CHA©) and using the insights to improve the next change implementation.
- Constantly communicating a clear and concise change message (what, why, benefits and WIIFM) with a feedback loop.
- Other enablers:
  - Developing a detailed programme change plan (PCP).
  - Stakeholder engagement and continued analysis and mapping.
  - Monitoring employee resistance.

Barriers:

- No change sponsor or one who is not effective and proactive in terms of constantly communicating the change strategy.
- Not starting to align employees, processes, systems and the leadership.
- No leadership support or a leadership team who are not effective and proactive change leaders.
- Failing to continue articulating a change vision.
- Not using a change management framework (or equivalent) to guide the change programme on critical elements such as assessing change history and preparing a detailed programme change plan.

- Thinking that achieving employee adoption is a singular process to implement successful sustainable change and the change team can be successful without sponsorship and leadership support.
- The leaders not engaging employees to articulate the change vision, so they understand the business reasons for this organisational change.
- Limited change communication using inadequate channels which allow rumours or misinformation to grow.
- Leaders thinking that a one-off change communication 'WIIFM' message will win over impacted stakeholders.
- Not assessing previous change for organisational learning and repeating the same change implementation failings.
- Other barriers:
  - No roadmap that communicates the high-level change plan and deliverables.
  - Not making provisions to reduce employee workload during change implementation.
  - A weak business case for change.
  - Thinking there will be no resistance.

Sponsor Role: During the **AUILM® Understanding** employee adoption step, the sponsor's main responsibility will be to continue with the three sub activities started in **Section 3.1.0**:

Say - Communicate the Change:

- **Articulate the Change Strategy**: Explaining to the employees how the change fits with the organisation's strategy.
- **Be the Face of the Change**: Ensuring that everyone in the organisation gets to hear and see the sponsor.
- **Communicate Constantly**: Communicate the right messages to the right stakeholders at the right time with a feedback loop.

3.2.1 Employee: How Will this Change Impact Me?

As part of understanding the change, employees want to know how it will impact them and why the organisation needs to implement the change

Having been made aware of the change, the employee will now want to further understand how it will impact them. The employee will want to understand why the organisation is making the change and how it will affect them in terms of job security, future role and ultimately their families. The quicker the employee starts to understand the change, the less likely they will be to disengage or develop resentment towards it.

Understanding answers the specifics about the change impact, how employees will be supported, timing, previous change experience, etc.

- ➢ **Understanding the Business Reasons for Change**: Some employees will want to gain an understanding of the business case for change and how it fits with the organisation's strategy.

- ➢ **Employee Change Impact and Support**: This describes how the change will impact the way employees work, their role, job description, department etc. This will include an understanding of changes to existing processes, systems and future support.

- ➢ **Implementation Timing**: Although employees may not want to know the details of the programme change plan (PCP), they will want an understanding of when it will impact them, key dates for communications, change design, training dates, go live, etc.

- ➢ **Previous Change History**: The employee's experience of previous organisational change, whether positive or negative, will input into their understanding of the current change.

3.2.2 Processes: Understand Why Processes Change

Business processes will always change and improve to make them more efficient, so they deliver better products and services

Business processes are continually improved to make them more efficient and effective, so they deliver better products, services or outcomes. Perform a value stream mapping (VSM) exercise on most organisation's 'As Is' key processes and you may be shocked by what the exercise uncovers. Typical inefficiencies might include:

- **High Waste**: Lean defines eight wastes commonly found in business, structured around acronym TIM H WOOD.
- **High Rework**: Correcting a defective or non-conforming part, product or service prior to customer delivery.
- **Long Lead-times**: The time required to produce a part, product or deliver a service.

This 'As Is' analysis can be used to design the new 'To Be' processes to reduce waste, lead-time and rework, etc. Analysis of the existing processes, either to improve or re-design them, usually requires the input of subject matter experts (SMEs). These SMEs can be existing employees who know the problems with the current processes.

Customers are continually expecting the latest technology and higher quality products and services delivered with shorter lead-times, as well as increased value. These external pressures mean organisations must continually improve their business processes to adapt to changing customer needs. Getting the employees to understand this and the necessity to change can greatly help them **Understand** the business case for change and quickly reduce resistance.

3.2.3 Systems: Understand Why Systems Change

4IR will change the way we work, new technology and AI will ensure business systems will continually improve and change

4IR will have a massive impact on organisations and how employees work. Employees will need to **Understand** that 4IR offers organisations two choices, either change the business or cease trading. Business management systems are continually evolving so they do more, meaning that fewer employees are required to run business operations. These systems can automate business processes, perform data analytics, make smarter decisions and enable better profits. With 4IR comes emerging technology breakthroughs such as:

➤ **Artificial Intelligence (AI)**: The ability of a computer, machine or robot to do tasks that are usually done by humans.

➤ **Autonomous Vehicles**: A driverless vehicle that is able to sense its environment and travel safely to a predetermined destination.

➤ **Three-Dimensional (3D) Printing**: An additive manufacturing process that creates a precise physical object from a digital design with almost no waste.

4IR will innovate and transform both business systems and processes. The technology will enable organisations to decrease costs, enhance customer experience, increase profits and enable organisations to sell more, innovate and remain relevant. Getting employees to **Understand** the implications of 4IR and the necessity to change can greatly help them to be less resistant about the future of work. A future in which organisations will require fewer employees, with more tasks being completed by systems and employees left to monitor and modify production processes.

3.2.4 Leadership: Creating Change Vision Understanding

Leaders need to develop a compelling change vision that inspires employees with purpose and is aligned to the organisation's strategy, values and beliefs

To support **AUILM® Understanding**, the leaders should continue their first critical responsibility, to '**Articulate** the change vision'. This builds on **Awareness**, explaining how the change is aligned to the organisation's strategy, vision, mission and objectives. Leaders should help employees understand why the change is important to the organisation, what the benefits are and the disadvantages of not implementing this change. The leaders of the organisation will not be able to help employees understand the need for change or enlist them without communicating an inspired change vision. The change vision needs to paint a mental picture of the future, a description of the future 'B' state. The vision is very important because leaders need to convey a vivid and attractive picture of what everyone is working towards in a clear, consistent and focused way, so that it inspires hope and helps employees understand how their work and future aligns with the change. It should describe a future that appeals to the employees on an emotional level, and it should create momentum and excitement, providing the required extra focus and motivation to implement the change.

Employees resist change because they don't understand what it will bring or think that it might have negative consequences for them. Leaders who passionately inspire a shared change vision make a positive difference to any change, transformation or improvement initiative. The change vision can become the heart and soul of the change, and it should be communicated consistently and relentlessly when and wherever possible.

3.2.5 a2BCMF® Step 3.1 Organisation Structure

To enable some change implementations, the organisation structure may also have to change, this can have unfavourable implications for other employees

Organisation structure is the third element of the change history assessment© (CHA©). Typically, when there are major changes to employee roles, processes and systems, these usually impact the organisation's structure which has to be modified to suit the way the organisation will operate in the future and make it effective. In many cases, the need to modify the organisation structure is not anticipated or planned for. It is only when the change is implemented that some employees or functions struggle with change adoption because the organisation structure does not support the new way of working.

The CHA© asks questions about previous organisational structural modifications to gain change history insights and learning. These insights and learning can be invaluable in shaping the next change, as well as be a prompt to the wider change team to consider this element when developing the programme change plan (PCP).

- ➢ **Roles and Responsibilities**: Does the organisation have clear roles and responsibilities aligned with business objectives to help change success?

- ➢ **Effective Functions**: Do the functions within your organisation work effectively within the current structure to deliver business objectives and help change success?

- ➢ **Modified Structure**: During the last change in your organisation, was the existing structure modified to make the change successful?

3.2.6 a2BCMF® Step 3.2 Organisation Workload

Organisation change capacity and employee workload are ignored in change implementation, until they become the reason for failure

An organisation's capacity can be defined as the organisation's total workload for delivering normal day-to-day operations and change activities. If the organisation does not have change capacity, it is unlikely the employees will be able to take on any extra workload. Not getting this balance right will negatively impact employee change adoption success rates. Organisational workload is the sixth element of the change history assessment© (CHA©). The results from many CHA©s constantly highlight this as a challenge (**see Table 3.2.10**). The feedback from employees was that their workload was not considered when the organisation was implementing change. Specific feedback indicated that workload was not taken into account when learning new software, technology, systems, methods or processes. Employee workload and capacity for change should also be a big consideration for the wider change team. The CHA© tries to understand how the organisation has addressed workload during change implementation:

> **Workload Considerations**: Was the existing employee workload considered when previous changes were implemented in the organisation?

> **Can Take on Extra Workload**: Do employees have the capacity to take on more new work associated with the change, as well as their existing work?

> **Leaders Aware of Workload**: Are leaders aware of the employee's workload and it will be considered during the next organisational change?

3.2.7 a2BCMF® Step 4.1 Learning Plan

While adopting change it is important to learn the new skills, but sometimes the new behaviours are critical

The skills and behaviours learning plan (SBLP) is a component plan of the main programme change plan (PCP), prepared during **a2BCMF® Step 4 - Develop Detailed Change Plan**. This plan identifies skills and behaviours that will be required for the employees to adapt to the new way of working. It will be beneficial if there are major changes to the existing processes and systems, which might require intensive training to close skills and knowledge gaps. It will also help to secure the budget if the change team foresees learning or training as a major activity in terms of money, effort and time. Some of the key elements of the SBLP are:

- **Setting Learning Objectives**: Clear learning objectives and training goals will make it easier to evaluate the training in terms of how it makes the change successful.

- **Training Needs Analysis (TNA)**: Used to identify skill and behaviour gaps between the current state 'a' and future state 'B'.

- **Training Project Planning**: Training can have a major impact on normal day-to-day operations and good planning can help to reduce organisation stress. Aligning training with the programme change plan (PCP) supports efficient change implementation.

- **Learning Budget**: Without acquiring a healthy budget, it is unlikely the training will be delivered as needed.

- **Other Considerations**: Training delivery format, follow-up coaching, tracking the right learning metrics, evaluation, etc.

3.2.8 a2BCMF® Step 4.2 Resistance Strategy Plan (RSP)

Even if a change is good for the organisation, some employees will resist, thus a resistance strategy should be planned

The resistance strategy plan (RSP) is a component plan of the main programme change plan (PCP) which is prepared during **a2BCMF® Step 4 - Develop Detailed Change Plan**. The RSP provides specific actions to understand and address resistance. The actions and plan focus on the change implementation strategy and vary depending on if it is a 'Tell' or 'Sell' change implementation approach. This plan may be needed if the change team foresees high resistance challenges from some groups of employees or other impacted stakeholders.

Defining and being prepared for employee change resistance will enhance the efficiency and effectiveness of the change approach. The main reasons for resistance will vary from organisation to organisation but typical reasons could include:

- **Lack of Change Awareness**: The less employees know about the change and its impact on them, the more fearful they will become.
- **Lack of Change Understanding**: Not understanding the business context or the urgency for the organisation to change.
- **Job Security**: Employees tend to resist any change that threatens their job security.
- **Fear of the Unknown**: The first thing any employee thinks about is how it could impact them and their family.
- **Low Trust**: If employees have low trust in the organisation and its leaders, they are unlikely to support the change.

3.2.9 a2B Change Management Framework® Steps 3 - 4

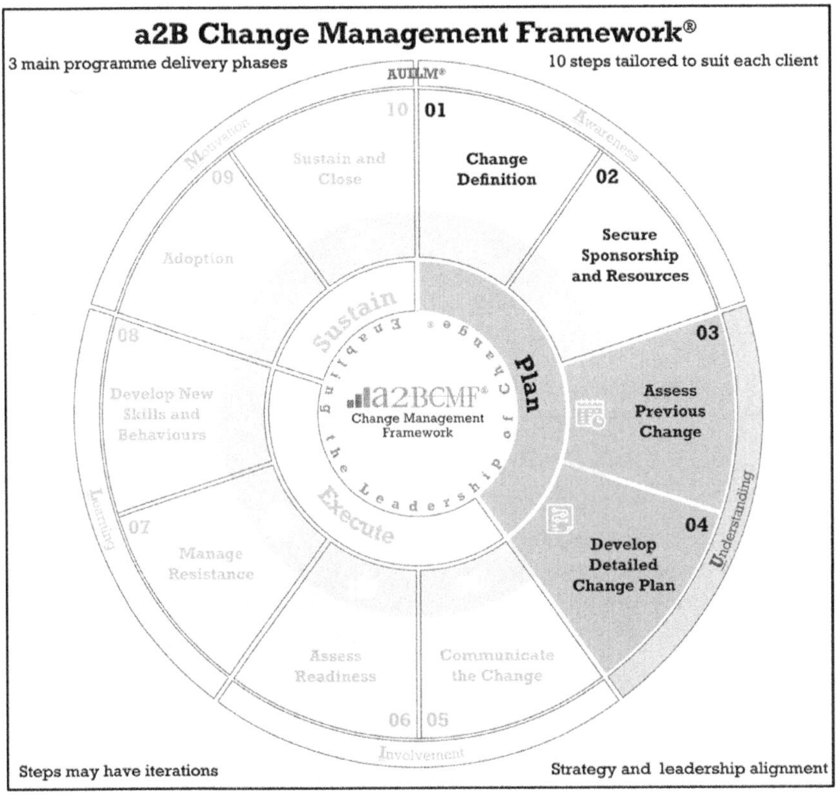

Figure 3.2.9 Change Management Framework® Steps 3 - 4

Adhering to **a2BCMF® Steps 3 and 4** can enhance employee change adoption and implementation success in the following ways:

> **Assess Previous Change**: A sign of organisational insanity is repeating the same failed change implementation approach and expecting employees to adopt the change. A change history assessment© (CHA©) can provide data and insights from previous change that could enhance future change implementation success.

> **Develop Detailed Change Plan**: Change management is a process that must be planned so it follows a structured approach, transiting the organisation from the current state 'a' to the future improved state 'B', aligning employees, processes and systems to achieve adoption and benefits realisation. This plan should, as a minimum, document the actions, timelines, milestones and resources needed to deliver successful change.

3.2 A**U**ILM® - Understanding

Table 3.2.10 below outlines some selected change concepts leaders of change should consider during the Plan phase (**see Change Management Handbook - Leadership of Change® Volume 3**).

a2B Change Management Framework® (a2BCMF®) Considerations
Step 3 - Assess Previous Change
Change History Assessment© (CHA©): Used to review the outcomes of previous change programmes and initiatives. It provides organisational insights that may increase the likelihood of successful implementation through the analysis of lessons learned, mitigating previous weaknesses and enhancing future success.
Step 4 - Develop Detailed Change Plan
Project Change Plan (PCP): The plan to deliver the change programme. It is structured around the ten-steps of the **a2BCMF®** and is important because it helps to ensure the change programme is delivered as planned, achieving employee change adoption and benefits realisation for the organisation. Depending on the complexity or challenges of the change programme and organisation structure, there may be a need for further component plans to be included in the main PCP.
Supporting Component Plans: Depending on the complexity or challenges of the change programme and organisation structure, there may be a need for further component plans to be included in the main PCP. Selected component plans can include the sponsorship and resource plan (SRP), resistance strategy plan (RSP), benefits plan and tracker (BPT), etc.
Resistance Strategy Plan (RSP): This component plan provides specific actions to understand and address resistance. This plan focuses on the change implementation strategy, which could be a '**Tell**' or '**Sell**'.

Table 3.2.10 Step 3 - 4 a2BCMF® Change Considerations

Section 3.3: Involvement - Execute Phase

3.3 AU**I**LM® - **I**nvolvement

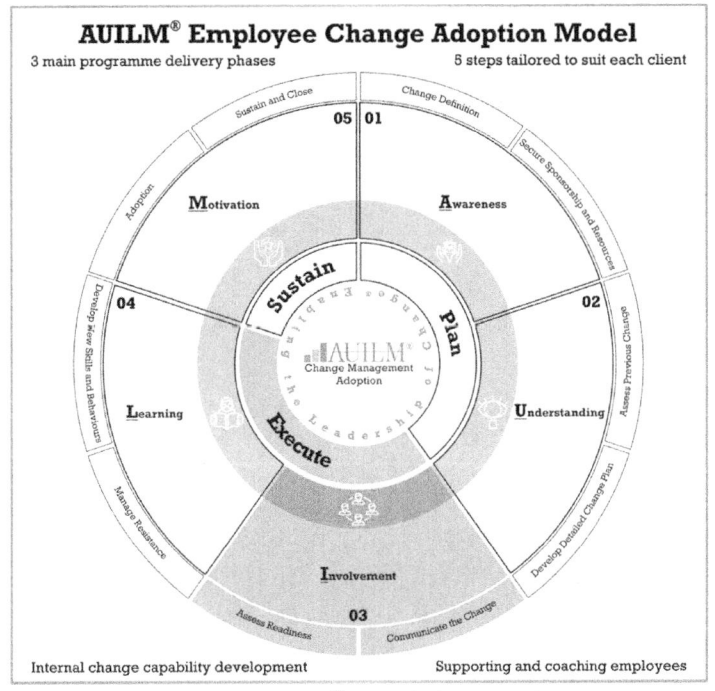

AUILM® Employee Change Adoption Model
3 main programme delivery phases — 5 steps tailored to suit each client

Internal change capability development — Supporting and coaching employees

Figure 3.3 AU**I**LM® Model - **I**nvolvement

Execute: Implementing the change into the organisation.

Section 3.3 **I**nvolvement - Structure

3.3.0 AUILM®: **I**nvolvement Overview.

3.3.1 Employee: Will I Be Involved?

3.3.2 Processes: Process Improvement Involvement.

3.3.3 Systems: System Improvement Involvement.

3.3.4 Leadership: Involved and Modelling the New Way.

3.3.5 a2BCMF® Step 5.1: Employee 1:1s.

3.3.6 a2BCMF® Step 5.2: Change Design Workshops.

3.3.7 a2BCMF® Step 6.1: Governance.

3.3.8 a2BCMF® Step 6.2: Culture.

3.3.9 a2BCMF® Figure: Steps 5 - 6.

3.3.10 a2BCMF® Table: Steps 5 - 6.

3.3.0 AU**I**LM®: **I**nvolvement Overview

Employees who are involved in the change design find it difficult to reject its implementation and become your major change agents, ensuring improved user adoption

Involvement: The third tactic focuses on involving the employee in the change directly. One of the biggest missed opportunities in major organisational change is not to get employees involved in shaping and designing the change. By maximising employee **Involvement** in influencing the change design prior to implementation, the organisation can both encourage improved change ownership and adoption. In fact, employees who are involved in the change design find it difficult to reject its implementation and become your major change agents, ensuring improved user adoption.

For this to happen, the leaders need to directly engage employees and infuse collaboration across the organisation, by clearly articulating their change vision, eradicating silos and other barriers. With the right preparation and environment, the change team can facilitate change design workshops with a relevant selection of employees who are subject matter experts (SMEs). Other benefits include:

> **Employee Engagement and Collaboration**: These are the foundations of change design involvement. By sharing the change design approach with employees, valuable feedback can be obtained.
> - o The objective of employee change engagement is to make them feel valued, motivated and committed so they positively contribute to organisational change success.

- o Collaboration enables good productivity and team working and is the primary factor which contributes to highly successful organisations.
- ➤ **Change Design Involvement**: The objective of these change workshops is to involve a selection of employees to co-design and test the change solutions with other selected impacted stakeholders.
- ➤ **Socialising the Change Design**: The proposed change design and approach can then be socialised with more employees to solicit feedback and harness valuable input which can help to shape the design further.

Importance of Employee Change Involvement

Employee change **Involvement** builds on the employee engagement from the **AUILM® Understand** step. By involving employees in the change, there is less chance of them becoming or feeling disconnected, either from the organisation or the change. In fact, the opposite happens. Employees who are involved in the change design start to trust the organisation, the leaders and the change. Collaborating with employees and keeping them involved in issues that affect them will reduce resistance and start to gain their buy-in to the change.

Benefits of Creating Employee Involvement:

- ➤ **Enhance Change Quality**: Involving selected employees in design and wider socialising will help to improve the change design solution and implementation approach.
- ➤ **Improved Change Acceptance and Adoption**: Employee change design involvement will greatly increase buy-in, change acceptance and improve user adoption.
- ➤ **Reduced Resistance**: Employee change design involvement not only makes it more difficult to reject its implementation, it also reduces resistance to implementation.

Enablers:

- ➤ Effective and proactive change sponsorship (**Support**).

- Aligning employees, processes, systems and the leadership.
- Effective and proactive change leadership (**Model**).
- Using the **a2B Change Management Framework**® to guide the change programme through **Step 5 - Communicate the Change** and **Step 6 - Assess Readiness**.
- Leadership continuing to articulate a change vision that is bold but realistic, which paints a vivid picture of the future state and appeals to the employee's hearts and minds.
- Stressing the importance of aligning the employee with the new processes and systems, supported by the organisational leaders.
- Performing a change readiness assessment (CRA) and (if required) resolving corrective actions before implementing change.
- Constantly communicating the change programme's progress, milestones achieved, etc to the impacted stakeholders with a feedback loop.
- Other enablers:
  - Communicating change progress using a wide range of media with feedback loops.
  - Ongoing stakeholder engagement, analysis and mapping.
  - Directly engaging with employee resistance to reduce it.

Barriers:

- No change sponsor or one who is not effective and proactive in terms of providing resources and engaging the organisation.
- Not creating an understanding of why employees, processes, systems and the leadership should be aligned.
- No leadership support or a leadership team who are not effective and proactive change leaders modelling the new way.
- Not using a change management framework or equivalent to guide the change programme on critical elements such as communicating the change and assessing readiness.

- Thinking that achieving employee adoption is a singular process to implement successful sustainable change and does not need the direct involvement of a sponsor and the leadership team.
- The leaders not having a change vision or having one that does not make the employees want to get involved in the change.
- Failing to constantly communicate change progress using multiple channels with a feedback loop or socialising the change design.
- The sponsor not ensuring that the leaders release quality resources to the change programme when required.
- The sponsor and leaders not getting actively involved in the change design.
- Other barriers:
  - Not having a detailed change communication plan (CCP) that depicts the key communications, channels and the timing of key messages or events.
  - Not performing a change readiness assessment (CRA) prior to change implementation.
  - Ignoring existing employee subject matter expertise and not considering it in the change design.
  - Thinking that because the leaders are involving the employees in the change design there will be no resistance.
  - Thinking that stakeholder identification, analysis and mapping is a one-off activity.

Sponsor Role: Having an effective and proactive sponsor becomes more important during the **AUILM® Involvement** employee adoption step. The sponsor's main responsibility moves from **Say** (communicating) to **Support** (actively involved) with the following three sub activities:

Support - Provide Resources, Engage and Coach:

- Provide quality resources.
- Engage the organisation.
- Develop change capability.

3.3.1 Employee: Will I Be Involved?

Without employee involvement in change design, there is little ownership or adoption

Employees who are involved in the change design will find it difficult to reject its implementation. They can become your major change agents, ensuring improved user adoption. By involving employees there is less chance of them becoming or feeling disconnected from the organisation and the change. Keeping them involved in issues that affect them will reduce resistance and start to gain their buy-in to the change. Selected employees with subject matter expertise (SME) can provide invaluable input into the change design and feedback can then be captured by socialising the change design with as many employees as possible. Selected advantages and benefits of involving employees in the change design are:

➢ **Enhance Change Success**: Employee input can sometimes be overlooked, but it can be invaluable and usually improves implementation success:
  o Enhanced change design quality and acceptance.
  o Improved employee change adoption and sustainability.

➢ **Positive Change Experience**: Engaging employees in the change design process makes the change experience much more pleasant:
  o Employees feel empowered as they help to shape the change, as opposed to the change being forced unto them.
  o Reduced personal stress and a greater sense of control.

3.3.2 Processes: Process Improvement Involvement

If properly facilitated, employees with subject matter expertise can provide invaluable input into designing the new processes

Clearly defined processes allow organisations to consistently produce quality work and products, which should increase customer satisfaction and profits. Inversely, processes with variation and waste cause customer complaints due to poor product quality or bad service. As employees work on an organisation's processes day in and day out, they become subject matter experts (SMEs) and they know the waste, rework, lead-times, etc. These SMEs are best placed to provide invaluable input into modifying or redesigning the new processes and behaviours. Their knowledge and expertise can be accessed by the change team in facilitated change design workshops. The SMEs should provide input into how the change should be implemented in terms of aligning the employees, processes and systems. While employee involvement in the change design will take time, the benefits of their engagement will usually outweigh the extra time and energy required. Employee change design involvement should be seen as an integral part of managing change. Socialising the output of the change design workshops to gain wider organisation feedback could enhance the design further and improve change implementation success.

The SMEs can also provide input into the training of the new processes. Additionally, given the right training (train-the-trainer), these SMEs can become classroom trainers and on-the-job coaches. However, there can be some disadvantages. The SMEs can be set in their ways, with strong inflexible opinions that might create negative feelings with some of the change team and fellow employees.

3.3.3 Systems: System Improvement Involvement

4IR technology advancement enhances business systems, internal capability may not always keep up

4IR offers employees two choices, either change or regress. Organisations and employees should see improving and changing systems as a fantastic opportunity to learn and grow, by getting involved in the change design process. The existing employees of an organisation will know the current system's performance deficiencies. These employees can provide invaluable insights in how to make the new systems better when they are involved in their implementation. This is particularly the case when an existing system is being updated and the employees know the system well. They will also have insights from previous system change implementations and they will know what works and what does not.

However, organisations usually buy their business systems from leading technology vendors who have their own SMEs, and it is unlikely that the organisation implementing the change will have the skills and knowledge to operate a brand-new system without extensive training and work experience. Business system design and capability are advancing at a fast rate and the existing internal SMEs may not have the required aptitude (even with training) to competently operate the new systems. That aside, some of the existing business SMEs can play a critical role in change design implementation:

- **System Integration**: Existing SMEs will be best placed to advise the vendor on system integration, legacy systems, etc.
- **Change Implementation**: The SMEs can advise on the best way to approach the change in terms of employee adoption.

3.3.4 Leadership: Involved and Modelling the New Way

The organisation will adopt change when the leaders are fully involved, and they model the new way

To achieve successful change implementation, the leaders must ensure employee **Involvement** in the change design and that they start to model the new way of working. More importantly, the employees need to see this. Modelling the new way of working is the one key task leaders of change do not need props for, nor can they delegate this task to others. They must free up time from normal day-to-day operations to be involved in the change design and then socialise it to get wider feedback. This starts with leaders being involved in the selection of employees with the right subject matter expertise (SME) who will provide input during the change design workshops. The leaders must also open and close these workshops, providing input and feedback throughout the design process. Similarly, they will need to be visible and actively involved during wider socialisation of the change design.

Leaders must also execute their second main responsibility, '**Model** the new way'. The organisation and its employees are more likely to adopt change when leaders show and model the new way. Selected benefits of getting leaders involved and modelling the new way are:

> **Collaborative One Team Mindset**: Successful change implementation requires a 'one team mindset', involvement and collaboration to achieve the main goals of full employee adoption, sustainable change and benefits realisation.

> **Setting the New Way and Standard**: Leaders who model the new way set the standard for change adoption and successful sustainable change. This standard starts to form when the leaders are actively involved in the change design.

3.3.5 a2BCMF® Step 5.1 Employee 1:1s

Employee 1:1s are a valuable leader and manager tactic and the first step in building a trusting relationship across the organisation

Employee 1:1s are a valuable tactic and the first step in building a trusting relationship. They offer the opportunity for leaders or managers to ask probing questions, sense body language and gauge responses. While face-to-face communication can be one of the most powerful channels (if used right), it requires a lot of effort and time. 1:1s should be positioned as a rich, relaxed and open conversation to discuss change implementation challenges and explore improvement opportunities, they should not be an interrogation. Some employees, managers and leaders may be anxious about having an honest 1:1 discussion but there are many benefits:

> **Direct Change Implementation Feedback**: 1:1s provide the change team with access to unfiltered feedback about the change which is not possible with group meetings.

> **Employee Involvement Reduces Resistance**: 1:1s provide the opportunity for the wider change team to show empathy when the employees share their feelings and concerns about the change. Addressing these concerns will build trust, as well as reduce blind or emotional resistance.

> **Builds Employee Trust and Collaboration**: 1:1 employee engagement is an important everyday activity in an organisation and directly impacts performance, employee attrition, customer satisfaction, revenue, profitability, etc. Employee change engagement is a critical factor in implementing successful organisational change.

3.3.6 a2BCMF® Step 5.2 Change Design Workshops

Enhance organisation change adoption and solution quality by getting employee input into the change design and then socialising the output

Change design workshops are a great way to get the employee involved in designing and shaping the change. The objective of these workshops is to co-design and test the change solutions with selected stakeholders and employees. There are many different ways of structuring these workshops, but a typical approach is for the change team or change agents to facilitate the event to support the work stream lead(s). The work stream lead and members of their team present their draft solutions or deliverables to obtain design input, gauge acceptance and avoid potential resistance.

Some organisations use the co-design concept to design the material to support the development of the new skills and behaviours (**a2BCMF® Step 8**). Consistent feedback from the change history assessment© (CHA©) indicates that employees are usually not involved in shaping the change but want to be. As well enhancing the employee change experience, the main advantages of involving employees in the change design process are:

- ➢ **Improved Solution Quality and Implementation**: Using employees who are SMEs of both processes and systems can provide insights into the organisation to improve design quality, change implementation approach, training material content, etc.

- ➢ **Employee Involvement Reduces Resistance**: Employees who are involved in the change design or who have provided input find it difficult to reject its implementation and become your major change agents, ensuring improved user adoption.

3.3.7 a2BCMF® Step 6.1 Governance

Independent change programme governance and oversight should ensure the leaders adhere to all change adoption steps and not falsely declare an early victory

Governance is the decision-making process, applied by authorised individuals or teams, for approving/rejecting, monitoring and adjusting activities of the programme change plan (PCP). It covers the systems and methods of how the change programme will be authorised, monitored and supported by its sponsoring organisation. The objective of governance is to have independent oversight of the change programme, as well approving budget, resources, activities, deliverables, approving each change **AUILM®** and **a2BCMF®** step, etc.

There are numerous reasons why many change programmes encounter problems or fail to achieve adoption and benefits realisation. Often strong independent governance and oversight could have prevented many problems from occurring. Effective governance includes:

➢ Establishing clear procedures and structures as to how the sponsoring organisation will oversee the change and its degree of autonomy.

➢ Ensuring that the goals of the change programme are aligned with the strategic vision, business case and resources.

➢ Identifying and nominating the sponsor.

➢ Authorising the programme budget and resources.

➢ Approving each change **AUILM®** and **a2BCMF®** step and allowing the programme to move to the next stage.

3.3.8 a2BCMF® Step 6.2 Culture

You cannot implement a change into an organisation that runs counter to its culture without focusing on behaviour change

An organisation's culture can enable change success or act as a barrier. Culture is a significant factor which needs to be considered when undertaking organisational change. Culture can be defined as a system of shared assumptions, values and beliefs, which govern how people behave. These shared values have a strong influence on employees in the organisation and dictate how they behave, act and perform their jobs. It is sometimes referred to as 'the way things are done around here'.

Cultural configurations do not always match or support an organisation's change strategy. Change teams, leaders and the sponsor can underestimate how much a strategy's effectiveness and any desired change depends on cultural alignment. Leaders often try to implement a change that is opposed by the deep-rooted practices and attitudes of an organisation's culture. However, for the change team to be successful, they may need to work within the organisation's culture. Culture trumps strategy every time. A typical approach could be:

➢ Assess and understand the current organisational culture.

➢ Define what the organisational culture should look like to support change success.

➢ Create and implement changes to reach the desired organisational culture, if required.

➢ Align the new employee behaviours with the new defined culture.

3.3.9 a2B Change Management Framework® Steps 5 - 6

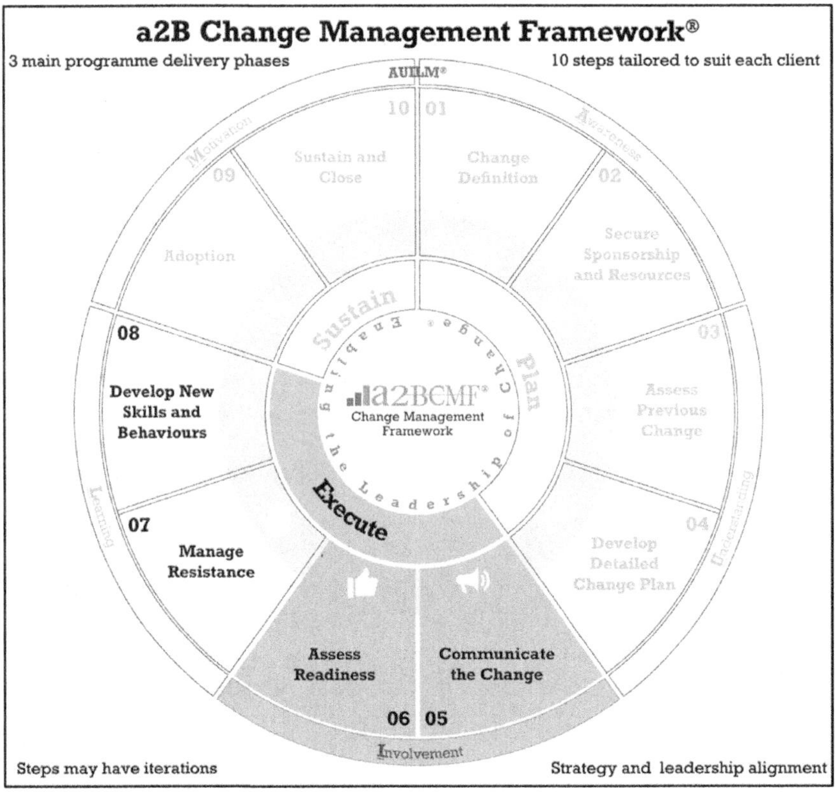

Figure 3.3.9 Change Management Framework® Steps 5 - 6

Adhering to **a2BCMF® Steps 5 and 6** can enhance employee change adoption and implementation success in the following ways:

> **Communicate the Change**: Effective change communication is about getting the right message to the right stakeholders at the right time, in their frame of reference with a feedback loop. Without constant two-way communication to the impacted stakeholders, they will become disconnected, resistance will build, and employee change adoption will become more difficult.

> **Assess Readiness**: Readiness is about ensuring the sponsor and leadership get the organisation and its employees ready so that resistance is limited, and adoption is maximised. Implementing change without checking if the organisation and employees are ready will probably limit the chances of successful change.

3.3 AUILM® - Involvement

Table 3.3.10 below outlines some selected change concepts leaders of change should consider during the Execute phase (**see Change Management Handbook - Leadership of Change® Volume 3**).

a2B Change Management Framework® (a2BCMF®) Considerations
Step 5 - Communicate the Change
Communication Planning Guide: The communication planning process defines the communication strategy and the best methods to deliver timely and useful information to various impacted stakeholders.
Why Are We Changing Guide: This concept addresses typical questions the impacted stakeholders ask when they become involved in an organisational change. It helps to create key communication text that answers these questions in a concise and consistent way.
Change Communication Plan (CCP): A formal and approved document designed to guide the execution and control of all change communications. It is a key enabler to change success and one of the most important documents within the change programme.
Step 6 - Assess Readiness
Change Readiness Assessment (CRA): An assessment to establish if the employee and organisation are ready for change implementation. It can also gauge whether resistance will be high or low. The CRA is used by the change team to gauge the organisation and the employee's readiness to implement the change.

Table 3.3.10 Steps 5 - 6 a2BCMF® Change Considerations

Section 3.4: <u>L</u>earning - Execute Phase

3.4 AUI**L**M® - **L**earning

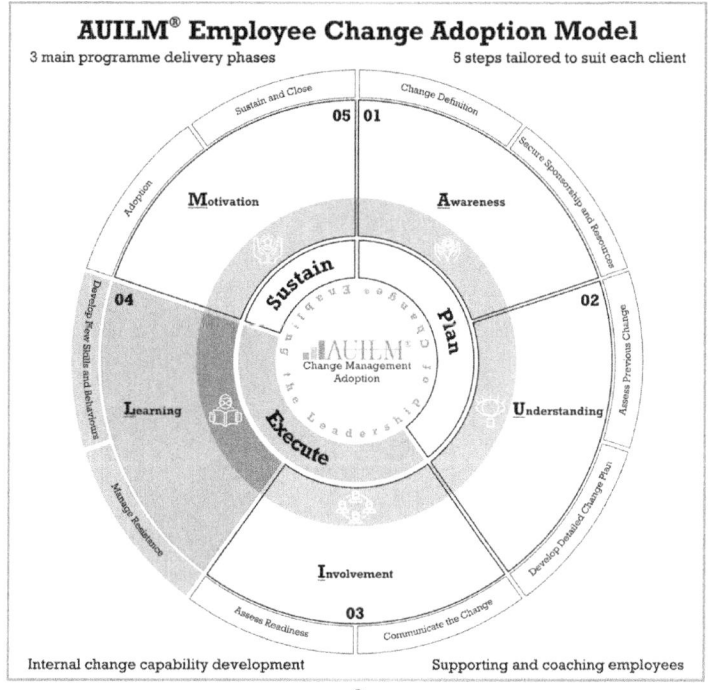

Figure 3.4 AUIL**M® Model - **L**earning**

Execute: Implementing the change into the organisation.

Section 3.4 **L**earning - Structure

3.4.0 AUIL**M®**: **L**earning Overview.

3.4.1 Employee: Learning the New Skills and Behaviours.

3.4.2 Processes: Learning the New Processes.

3.4.3 Systems: Learning the New Systems.

3.4.4 Leadership: Learning and Modelling the New Way.

3.4.5 a2BCMF® Step 7.1: Resistance Tipping Point.

3.4.6 a2BCMF® Step 7.2: Implementation Approaches.

3.4.7 a2BCMF® Step 8.1: Develop New Skills.

3.4.8 a2BCMF® Step 8.2: Develop New Behaviours.

3.4.9 a2BCMF® Figure: Steps 7 - 8.

3.4.10 a2BCMF® Table: Steps 7 - 8.

3.4.0 AUILM®: Learning Overview

While adopting change, it is important to learn the new skills, but sometimes the new behaviours are critical

Learning: The fourth tactic is about getting the employee to see the change as an opportunity for **Learning** and growth. This step focuses on ensuring the employee develops the new skills and behaviours for them to operate proficiently so the change is successful. If the employee has successfully transitioned through **AUILM® Awareness**, **Understand** and **Involvement** steps they should be well prepared to take on the new learning.

Growth mindset employees will see any new change as a positive, personal development opportunity for learning. The employees must be supported by the organisation and its leaders to develop new competencies, so they have the capability and confidence to operate the new way of working. Developing the new skills and behaviours usually requires a structured design approach, a scheduled training plan which is coordinated with change implementation (go-live) and coaching, as well as an appraisal to check effectiveness:

- ➢ **Detailed Training Design**: There must be a structured process to define the training objectives, identify the new skills and behaviours, evaluate existing skills and behaviours and then assess which training courses would best close the gaps.

- ➢ **Training**: Training is used to develop skills and is usually required for changes in processes, procedures, systems, the introduction of new technology, etc.

- ➢ **Coaching**: On site coaching will sometimes be needed to compliment and reinforce the training, it will help some employees to refine and develop the skills that have not been fully learned during training.

Importance of Employee Change Learning

Without learning new skills and behaviours, the employee will not be able to proficiency operate the new processes and systems to improve operating performance. Training cannot ever be optional and current employee workload should be reduced to make the learning successful. No matter how good the new processes or how advanced the new systems are, without matching operator competency, organisation performance could be negatively impacted.

Benefits of Creating Employee Learning:

- **Adopt the New Way of Working**: The employee will have to develop the new skills and behaviours to adopt the new way of working.

- **Working Alignment of Employees, Processes and Systems**: If the previous **AUILM**® steps have properly been considered, the alignment of employees, processes and systems should be staring to work proficiently and in unison as learning progresses.

- **Improved Operating Performance**: The new way of working with the aligned employees, processes and systems should improve operating performance, deliver better products and services, beat the competition, etc. The tangible and intangible benefits should then start to be realised.

Enablers:

- Continued effective and proactive change sponsorship (**Support**).

- Ensuring that training stresses the importance of employee, processes, systems and leadership alignment.

- Continued effective and proactive change leadership (**Model**).

- Using the **a2B Change Management Framework**® to guide the change programme through **Step 7 - Manage Resistance** and **Step 8 - Develop New Skills and Behaviours**.

- Leadership continuing to articulate the change vision that appeals to the employee's hearts and minds and explaining how learning the new skills and behaviours fits with the future state.
- More focused engagement on employees from the '**Observer**' and '**REBEL**' groups to reduce any potential resistance.
- Ensuring the importance of exhibiting the right employee behaviour is not ignored during skills and knowledge training.
- Monitoring and tracking the training plan to ensure progress is kept to schedule, KPIs are on target, employee feedback is positive, etc.
- Other enablers:
  - Constantly communicating the change programme's progress, milestones achieved, etc to the impacted stakeholders with a feedback loop.
  - Continued ongoing stakeholder engagement, analysis and mapping.
  - Identifying employees, stakeholder groups, functions or departments where an important intervention may have to be made by the change team to ensure successful change implementation.

Barriers:

- No change sponsor or one who is not effective and proactive in terms of being involved in learning and coaching activities.
- Not stressing, during training, the importance of aligning employees, processes, systems and the leadership.
- A leadership team who are not effective and proactive change leaders modelling the new skills and behaviours.
- Not using a change management framework or equivalent to guide the change programme on critical elements, such as managing resistance and developing the new skills and behaviours.
- Thinking that achieving employee adoption is a singular process to implement successful sustainable change without direct learning input from the sponsor and leadership team.

- The leaders not having a change vision or articulating one that is not realistic or does not explain why learning the new skills and behaviours are so important for change adoption.
- The sponsor and leaders not showing up at the training sessions.
- Failing to constantly communicate change and training progress using multiple channels with a feedback loop.
- The sponsor and leaders not ensuring post training on-site follow-up coaching is used to close any competency gaps.
- Other barriers:
  - Not selecting the appropriate change implementation approach: '**Tell**' versus '**Sell**'.
  - Not having a resistance strategy plan (RSP) when strong employee resistance was anticipated.
  - Ceasing stakeholder analysis and mapping too early.
  - Not using the change agents and '**Advocates**' to positively impact the '**Observers**' and '**REBELs**'.
  - Not using a structured approach to develop the new skills: Define, Identify, Evaluate, Assess, Deliver (Coach) and Appraise the training (**a2BDNS© Model - see Section 3.4.7**).
  - Thinking organisational change can be successful without a focus on employee behaviour change.

Sponsor Role: The need for a effective and proactive sponsor during **AUILM® Learning** continues to ramp up in terms of importance. The three sub activities of **Support** are vital for **Learning** success:

Support: Provide Resources, Engage and Coach:

- **Provide Quality Resources**: Continue to ensure the employee's workload is reduced while they are released for training.
- **Engage the Organisation**: Continue to engage the organisation, especially around training and coaching progress.
- **Develop Change Capability**: Continue to coach the organisation to develop change capability to support ongoing change implementation.

3.4.1 Employee: Learning the New Skills and Behaviours

Preparing for the new way of working requires employees with a growth mindset to learn the new skills and the associated behaviours

Learning the new skills and behaviours is a major milestone for impacted employees during change implementation. For most, this is usually a positive experience and a chance to develop personally. However, some employees can get quite anxious thinking about having to learn new processes and systems. Some will worry that they will not be able to acquire the new skills and behaviours, and a few will panic, worrying that this might mean they may not have a job in the future. It is very important that the wider change team provides all employees with the confidence that they will be supported to learn the new skills and behaviours throughout the change journey. Even if there are classroom learning gaps, on-the-job coaching will be used to close these gaps. This is not always practical, but at the early stages of learning it is usually the best strategy.

Fixed and growth mindsets will come into play and determine how well an employee is likely to adapt to learning the news skills and behaviours. Employees with a fixed mindset will, by default, reject and resist disruption and change. This will prevent learning. Their assumption is that change is usually always bad, and they stick what they know. However, growth mindset employees embrace change to improve organisation performance with no wasted time spent on resisting inevitable change. Some growth mindset attributes that can benefit the change team are:

➢ Embrace organisational change and adopt the new way.

➢ Talents can be developed through learning and hard work.

3.4.2 Processes: Learning the New Processes

Learning new processes requires both experiential learning to develop the skills, the 'how', as well as theoretical knowledge, the 'what'

Process training comprises a series of steps that need to be followed systematically to create an efficient training programme. This systematic approach to training ensures that employees are prepared for the new way of working. They should have the new skills and behaviours to operate proficiently so the change is successful. Training should focus on both the skills (how) and the required theoretical knowledge (what). Other considerations include:

- **Training Material and Props**: How will this be created? Will the internal training department be the main author? Will it be contracted out? Will internal subject matter experts (SMEs) be involved in creating and delivering the training?
- **Operator Work Instructions**: Who will create and own the new standard work instructions (SWI) or equivalent?
- **Training Delivery**: Who will deliver the training and how will the employee's skills be assessed post training?
    - **Classroom or Online**: What type of facilities are needed?
    - **On-the-Job Training**: Will this impact day-to-day operations?
- **Follow-up Coaching**: Will coaching be used to close identified skills and knowledge gaps?
- **Training Evaluation**: How will effectiveness be evaluated?
- **Future Employee On-boarding**: How will new employees be on-boarded and who will own the training material?

3.4.3 Systems: Learning the New Systems

An organisation's ability to develop new employee system competency and use it, will provide competitive advantage

It can be a major challenge to 'go-live' with a new system, but it is often a bigger issue to get the training right. Organisations often underestimate the importance, complexity, or budgets that it takes to provide effective training. Getting good trainers, ensuring employees are released for the training and ensuring it is delivered when required are other challenges. Other considerations include:

- **System Training Material**: Will the material be supplied by the vendor or will it be created internally?
- **System Operating Manual**: Will the vendor's system operating manual (SOM) be used? How will it be integrated into the organisation? How will vendor SOM updates be controlled?
- **Training Delivery**: Who will deliver the training? How will the employee's skills be assessed post training?
  - **On-line or Classroom**: What type of facilities are needed?
- **Follow-up Superuser Coaching**: Will superuser coaching be used to close identified system skills and knowledge gaps?
  - **Superuser Selection**: Will the superusers be recruited or will the organisation train existing SMEs?
- **Training Evaluation**: How will effectiveness be evaluated?
- **Future Employee On-boarding**: How will new employees be on-boarded? Will employees need to have industry recognised qualifications?

3.4.4 Leadership: Learning and Modelling the New Way

Leaders of change must model the new skills and behaviours and then support the employees to learn them

Organisational and employee learning is an important factor when implementing change. An organisation's ability to enable its employees to learn new skills and behaviours will have a major positive impact on change implementation. It will also give the organisation a competitive advantage. The proactive involvement of the leadership team in the development of an employee's new skills and behaviours will support change adoption, as well as benefits realisation. During the new skills development process, the employees should know that the leaders are fully embedded in the design, delivery and appraisal of training.

The leaders must continue to execute their second main responsibility, '**Model** the new way'. When the leaders model the new skills and behaviours it sets a standard that all employees should follow. Equally, if a single leader fails to model the new way, they give some employees an excuse to resist adoption. Modelling the new learning and being actively involved in the learning could include the following leadership activities:

- Be seen to attend some of the new skills and behaviour training, similar to what the employees are attending.
- Open and close the employee training sessions and outline the importance of learning the new skills and behaviours.
- Review the feedback forms from the training sessions and intervene if required.
- Protect the training and coaching budgets from being reduced due to overspend in other change programme areas.

3.4.5 a2BCMF® Step 7.1 Resistance Tipping Point

There are 3 groups of employees in any change journey: 'Advocates', 'Observers' and 'REBELs'. Each reacts differently to organisational change and will have different levels of resistance

Change Resistance Employee Standpoints

"There are 3 groups of employees in any change journey: **'Advocates'**, **'Observers'** and **'REBELs'**. Each reacts differently to organisational change and will have different levels of resistance"

REBELs — Observers — Advocates

Individual Standpoints

Figure 3.4.5 Change Resistance Standpoints

Organisations should treat resistance as an integral part of delivering change. Resistance can be classified into three simple employee groups: **'Advocates'**, **'Observers'** and **'REBELs'**:

- ➤ **Advocates**: Tend to embrace and lead change within the organisation as they are more comfortable with it.
- ➤ **Observers**: Tend to monitor the **'Advocates'** and assess if the change is benefiting them.
- ➤ **REBELs**: Tend to resist change blindly, sometimes this can be a natural reaction even if the change is to their benefit.

The wider change team should support the change agents to work with the three main employee groups involved in change. Change agents and **'Advocates'** can be a powerful coalition, they can have a considerable positive impact on the other groups. Working together, they can help to find the **'Tipping Point'**, convincing the **'Observers'** to join them. Equally, the change agents can help reduce **'REBEL'** resistance, moving the **'REBELs'** to become **'Observers'**. Once the tipping point is reached an amazing phenomenon takes place, whereby more and more employees start adopting the new way of working, as well as embracing the change at an accelerated pace.

3.4.6 a2BCMF® Step 7.2 Implementation Approaches

Change Approach: If it is about compliance, legislation or safety it will be a 'Tell'. If it is about winning hearts and minds it will be a 'Sell'

Tell and Sell Change Implementation Approaches

Tell
- Quick implementation
- Little employee buy-in
- May fail long-term

Compliance

Sell
- Slow Implementation
- Gains employee buy-in
- Gains Adoption

Hearts and Minds

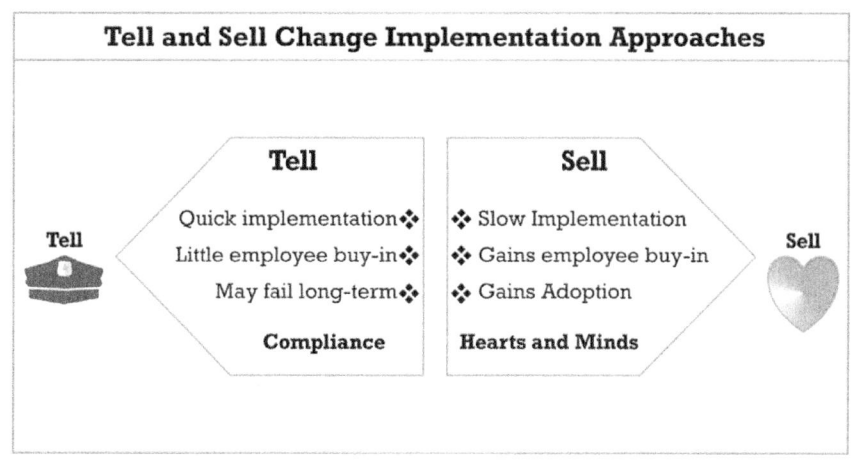

Figure 3.4.6 Change Implementation Approaches

The change implementation approach depends on the type of change. If the change is about compliance, legislation or safety it will be a '**Tell**'. If it is about winning hearts and minds it will be a '**Sell**'. Both approaches have advantages and disadvantages!

Tell: Compliance:

- **Advantages**: Speed is the nature of this type of change implementation. The organisation enforces the implementation decision, with consequences for those who do not conform.
- **Disadvantages**: Changes like this are implemented quickly with no time for staff consultation. As a result, employees will feel that this change is 'done unto them'.

Sell: Win heart and minds:

- **Advantages**: This type of change allows the organisation to communicate the change in advance, take feedback and gain staff buy-in, winning hearts and minds.
- **Disadvantages**: The process of communicating, involving lots of people and receiving feedback, takes time. This type of change approach takes a lot longer than the '**Tell**' approach and much more organisational effort.

3.4.7 a2BCMF® Step 8.1 Develop New Skills

Developing new employee skills is a structured process that requires follow-up coaching and leadership involvement throughout

Developing the New Skills Model (a2BDNS©)

1. Define	3. Evaluate	5. Deliver and Coach
Define the new skills and behaviour training objectives and align them with the change programme	Evaluate existing skills and behaviour traits for impacted employees using structured analysis to establish gaps	Deliver the skills training programmes to close the identified gaps. Follow-up with coaching

(i) Training Design — (ii) Competence Delivery

2. Identify	4. Assess	6. Appraise
Identify new skills and behaviours needed to meet objectives	Assess available courses or design new courses to close gaps in skill levels and behaviours	Appraise the new skills to establish the effectiveness of the training and coaching that is preparing the employees to operate at the future state 'B'

(iii) Training Appraisal

Developing the New Skills

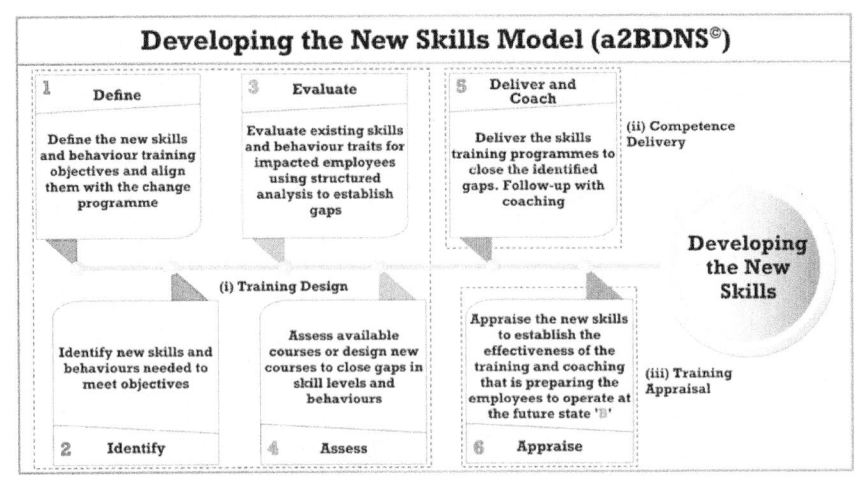

Figure 3.4.7 Develop New Skills

The **a2BDNS© Model** is a six-step process for developing the new skills, abilities and knowledge needed by the employees to perform their new tasks and activities when new processes and systems are introduced as part of the change. The old skills and knowledge should be leveraged as much as possible into the new training. The wider change team should approach the six steps of developing the new skills in three main phases:

➢ **Training Design 1 - 4**: Define, Identify, Evaluate and Assess.

➢ **Competency Delivery 5**: Deliver and Coach.

➢ **Training Appraisal 6**: Appraise.

This structured approach to developing new skills should be a collective process within change programmes, it needs to involve the employees, leaders and also the change team. Successfully developing the new skills is a critical enabler to change adoption. It must get the right level of focus and planned training budgets should be protected against the temptation of balancing overspend in other areas of the change programme. A change capable organisation understands its competitive advantage depends on its ability to learn at the same pace as, or faster than, change in its environment.

3.4.8 a2BCMF® Step 8.2 Develop New Behaviours

If you do not change employee behaviour, you will not get organisational change or performance improvement

a2B5R® Employee Behaviour Change Model

- ❖ Reinforce the new behaviours
- ❖ Recognise there is a behaviour problem
- ❖ Replicate the new behaviours
- ❖ Redesign the new solution
- ❖ Resolve to implement the new behaviours

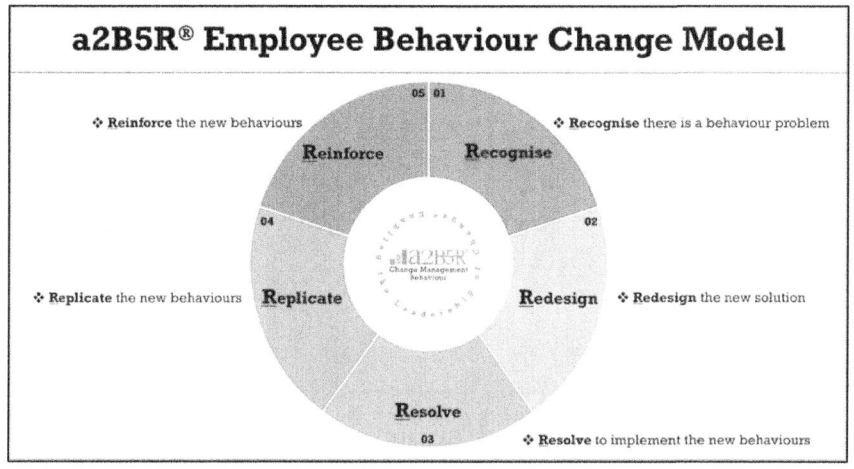

Figure 3.4.8 Develop New Behaviours

The **a2B5R® Behaviour Change Model** supports the change team to embed the few new behaviours that are critical to change success. In many instances, employee change adoption will not be achieved unless the employees make a behavioural change. This approach systematically supports the transition of the employee's behavioural change. The few new critical behaviours will have been defined during the definition step and they will be developed along with the new skills. There are five critical steps to support employee behavioural change:

> **Recognise**: The first tactic is to officially accept that there is a problem with the current behaviours within the organisation.

> **Redesign**: The second tactic is to agree to define the few new critical behaviours and to redesign a new solution.

> **Resolve**: The third tactic focuses on getting all employees to make a resolution to implement the few new critical behaviours.

> **Replicate**: The fourth tactic is about getting the employee to continue replicating the new behaviours.

> **Reinforce**: The final tactic focuses on ensuring the new behaviours are reinforced so they are embedded.

3.4.9 a2B Change Management Framework® Steps 7 - 8

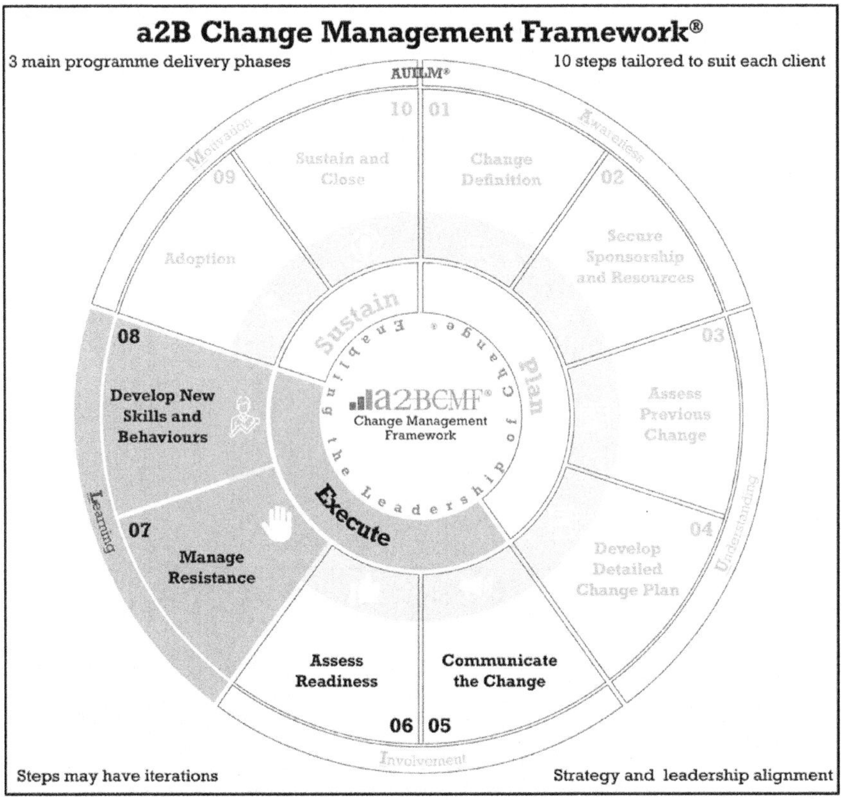

Figure 3.4.9 Change Management Framework® Steps 7 - 8

Adhering to **a2BCMF® Steps 7 and 8** can enhance employee change adoption and implementation success in the following ways:

> **Manage Resistance**: Change resistance is the reaction by the organisation, departments or individuals when they perceive that an organisational change coming their way could be a threat to them. It will trigger actions that negatively impact change implementation and adoption.

> **Develop New Skills and Behaviours**: Developing the employee's new skills and behaviours are critical enablers to successful employee adoption. A structured approach is required to develop the new skills and behaviours. If this is not completed properly, it is unlikely that the employee will be able to adopt of the new ways of working.

Table 3.4.10 below outlines some selected change concepts leaders of change should consider during the Execute phase (**see Change Management Handbook - Leadership of Change® Volume 3**).

a2B Change Management Framework® (a2BCMF®) Considerations
Step 7 - Manage Resistance
Resistance Groups: There are three organisational stakeholder groups that should be considered as part of resistance planning. If high resistance is anticipated, they should be considered as part of the stakeholder engagement plan.
Individual Reasons for Resistance: The change team should be aware of the most common reasons people resist change and what might be typical in their organisation. Resistance, for whatever reason, will negatively impact change implementation and adoption speed. There are ten typical employee reasons for resistance and associated actions to reduce this resistance.
Step 8 - Develop New Skills and Behaviours
Behaviour Change Challenge: The term employee behaviour refers to the way in which employees respond to specific circumstances or changes in the workplace. While many elements determine an individual's behaviour in the workplace, employees are shaped by the organisation's culture. The right employee behaviour is a key determinant of successful change and adoption of the new ways of working.
The Importance of New Skills and Behaviours: Developing effective skills and behaviours to deliver the new change is critical to support new processes, systems, technology, products, services, etc. When done properly, training facilitates change adoption and sustainable benefits.
Change Management Training: Organisations with internal change management capability have an advantage over their competitors. Having internal change management capability gives the organisation both agility and expertise to manage internal change. Change management programmes will be more effective if the key employees leading the change (change team, sponsor, change agents, etc) have similar change management training.

Table 3.4.10 Step 7 - 8 a2BCMF® Change Considerations

Section 3.5: <u>M</u>otivation - Sustain Phase

3.5 AUIL**M**® - **M**otivation

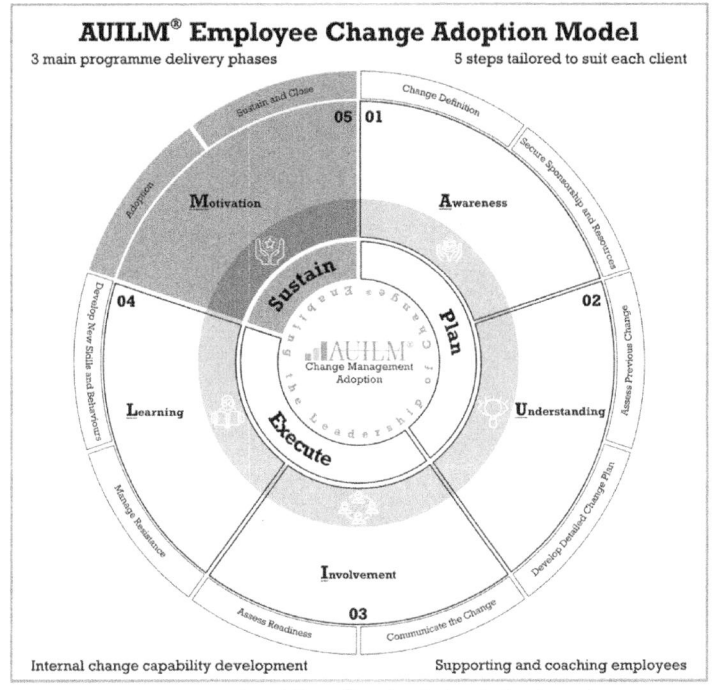

AUILM® Employee Change Adoption Model
3 main programme delivery phases — 5 steps tailored to suit each client

Figure 3.5 AUIL**M**® Model - **M**otivation

Sustain: Sustaining change adoption and benefits realisation.

Section 3.5 Motivation - Structure

3.5.0 AUILM®: **M**otivation Overview.

3.5.1 Employee: What Will keep Me Motivated?

3.5.2 Processes: Motivate to Ensure Process Adherence.

3.5.3 Systems: Motivate to Ensure System Compliance.

3.5.4 Leadership: Motivating and Intervening.

3.5.5 a2BCMF® Step 9.1: Change Adoption Assessment.

3.5.6 a2BCMF® Step 9.2: Growth Mindset.

3.5.7 a2BCMF® Step 10.1: Sustain the Change.

3.5.8 a2BCMF® Step 10.2: Close the Change Programme.

3.5.9 a2BCMF® Figure: Steps 9 - 10.

3.5.10 a2BCMF® Table: Steps 9 - 10.

3.5.0 AUILM®: Motivation Overview

For the change to become normal operations, the leadership needs to support the employees so they have the motivation and discipline to sustain the new way of working

Motivation: The final tactic focuses on ensuring **Motivation** for sustainable change after it is passed back to operations and the change team has dissolved. With new skills maturing and the new behaviours being reinforced, the final step is to make sure that employees remain motivated. This will ensure they are positively focused to do their part to improve organisation performance. An individual performance plan (IPP) and a linked reward mechanism to reinforce positive performance should be put in place.

Two typical performance reward mechanisms that organisations utilise are:

> **Individual Performance Plan (IPP)**: The IPP is an instrument that can be used to establish employee performance expectations, career development, etc. It can be used to directly link activities that support successful change with rewards.

> **Balanced Scorecard (BSC)**: The BSC translates a company's vision and strategy into a coherent set of performance measures. It can be repositioned as a change implementation tool, for the purpose of ensuring that change benefits are realised.

Importance of Employee Change Motivation

When the change programme closes, the change team dissolves and change ownership is transferred to operations. There needs to be motivation for the employee to continue using the new way of working. An incentive offered through the organisation's reward mechanism acts as the motivation to adopt and sustain the new way of working.

Benefits of Creating Employee Motivation:

- **Individual Performance Plan (IPP)**: When the change becomes normal day-to-day operations, it is extremely important that each and every employee's work activity is linked to the change. Most organisations cannot leave this to chance and the IPP, if properly implemented, can create the right motivation to ensure sustainable change.

- **Change Benefits Delivery Bonus**: Organisations often offer a collective annual bonus to share with all employees if the organisation delivers its strategic objectives. A collective bonus can motivate the entire organisation to work as one team to deliver the change programme's objective, benefits delivery, ROI and improved operating performance.

- **Embed as Normal Operations**: For the change to become normal day-to-day operations, it is extremely important that each and every employee's work activity is linked to this incentive. The organisation's reward mechanism acts as the motivation to embed the change as normal day-to-day operations.

Enablers:

- Effective and proactive change sponsorship (**Sustain**).
- Embedding the alignment of employees, processes, systems and the leadership.
- Effective and proactive change leadership (**Intervene**).
- Using the **a2B Change Management Framework**® to guide the change programme through **Step 9 - Adoption** and **Step 10 - Close and Sustain**.
- Sponsor and leaders intervening to ensure sustainable change.
- The sponsor and leaders offering small or token rewards to employees for behaviour change and adoption.

- Ensuring there is a controlled and formal process for the transfer of ownership to normal day-to-day operations.
- Officially closing the change programme with governance approval, closing administrative activities and then celebrating.
- Other enablers:
  - All employees intervening to ensure sustainable change and that the change is embedded as normal day-to-day business.
  - Recording lessons learned from the change programme so they will provide insights and value for future change programmes.
  - Aligning benefits realisation with future organisational performance measures.
  - Issuing a final change communication sharing results to date, ROI, how change benefits will be measured going forward, etc.

Barriers:

- The change sponsor losing focus, claiming early change successes and not executing the **Sustain** sponsor responsibilities of intervening, rewarding and embedding the change.
- Not embedding the alignment of employees, processes, systems and the leadership.
- Leadership losing focus, claiming early change successes and not executing their **Intervene** responsibility by being effective and proactive change leaders in terms of intervening to ensure sustainable change.
- Not using a change management framework or equivalent to guide the change programme on critical elements such as formally closing and sustaining the change.
- Thinking that achieving employee adoption is a singular process to implement successful sustainable change without a sponsor and leadership embedding the change as normal day-to-day operations.
- Having a superficial transfer of ownership from the change team to normal operations with no formal programme governance and approval.

- ➢ Letting the change team dissolve too quickly with open actions and administration issues still to be closed.
- ➢ Leaders thinking that because it appears the employees have adopted the change they can now focus on normal day-to-day operations.
- ➢ Not having a benefits delivery, transition and sustainment plan or process to ensure benefits realisation when the responsibility is transferred to operations.
- o Other barriers:
  - o Thinking that all employees will continue to sustain the new way of working after the change becomes embedded into normal day-to-day operations.
  - o Thinking that because change ownership has been formally handed to operations the benefits will be fully realised.
  - o Not linking change benefits delivery to the organisation's balanced scorecard (BSC) or employee's individual performance plan (IPP).
  - o Thinking the next change will be 'easy', rather than 'easier'.

Sponsor Role: This final responsibility is the most important of them all. During the **AUILM® Motivation** employee adoption step, the sponsor's main responsibility and sub activities will be:

<u>S</u>ustain - Intervene, Reward and Embed:

- **Intervene to Sustain the Change**.
- **Reward Change Behaviour and Adoption**.
- **Embed as Normal Operations**.

This is a precautious step in the change programme life cycle and unless the final activities are put in place, all the good work of the implementation could be lost. The sponsor and the overall governance need to confirm the change is closed using a controlled process with formal approval to ensure the employees do not revert to the old way of working.

3.5.1 Employee: What Will keep Me Motivated?

For the change to become normal operations, leadership needs to support the employees so they have the motivation and discipline to sustain the new way of working

The final adoption tactic focuses on ensuring employee motivation for sustainable change after the change is passed back to operations and the change team has dissolved. With new skills maturing and the new behaviours being reinforced, the final step is to make sure that employees remain motivated, and the change is embedded as normal day-to-day operations.

An individual performance plan (IPP) is an instrument that can be used to establish performance expectations and to support performance evaluation, as well as the career development of each employee. It can be a powerful vehicle to support change implementation by aligning employee performance to change and benefits realisation. It should define the skills and behaviours expected so that the employee can adopt the change. It should also be linked directly to the organisation's balanced scorecard (BSC) to show the employee how their individual performance supports the change programme. The BSC can measure benefits realisation post change programme closure. The BSC can also directly link to each employee's IPP and their bonus and recognition rewards. The IPP normally contains the following:

➢ Specific goals for learning and development.

➢ Individual key performance measures.

➢ A link to the organisation's key performance measures.

➢ Actions required to achieve goals.

3.5.2 Processes: Motivate to Ensure Process Adherence

Why do employees act surprised when there are defects, rework or unhappy customers when process steps are not adhered to?

Ensuring process compliance can be a challenge in any organisation. Processes are the foundation of how the organisation operates and how it achieves its objectives to deliver value. Unfortunately, many organisations do not give processes enough focus. Too many employees nonchalantly follow process instructions, deciding which steps they will adhere to and how much effort they will expel. Worse still, employees detach their work input from the process output, causing defects, poor customer services, etc. Leaders must ensure that employees adhere to process instructions. Leaders must ensure employees are **Motivated** and they **Intervene** when necessary to ensure sustainable change. Root causes of non-compliance can be:

- ➢ **Change Readiness Assessment**: It was not executed, or the results were ignored, but the leaders proceeded regardless.
- ➢ **Business Process Understanding**: Lack of focus on the importance of business processes and alignment.
  - o **Organisation Culture**: Departments and employees working in silo cultures and not maximising the process value chain.
  - o **Process Instructions**: Process instructions, procedures and other job aids not visually located within the workplace.
- ➢ **Training Programme**: Not properly coordinated and managed.
  - o **Missed Training**: Employees did not attend training.
- ➢ **No Post Training Assessment or Coaching**: There was no assessment to verify or close skills and knowledge gaps.

3.5.3 Systems: Motivate to Ensure System Compliance

There are few occasions when employees circumvent business systems where it does not cause rework, quality or finance problems and customer dissatisfaction

Many organisations do not achieve the ROI that new business systems promise. There is a tendency for some employees to revert back to rogue management tools (spreadsheets, etc.) when there are operational disruptions, the system seems too complex, or the training failed. Typical employee excuses for circumventing the system include counterintuitive screen functionality, confusing navigation, an illogical system, or a poor training instructor. Even when business systems have far superior capability, some employees will revert back to the old way or not use the system as intended. The leaders must ensure they **Motivate** and **Intervene** when employee compliance is lacking, to ensure sustainable change. Root causes of non-compliance can be:

➤ **Change Readiness Assessment**: It was not performed, or the negative results were ignored, and the leaders still proceeded.

➤ **Role Assessment**: The job description, competencies and selection processes were not properly considered.

  o **Learning Growth Mindset**: Existing employees were selected but were not active learners (fixed mindset).

  o **Lack of Technical Skills**: The role requires knowledge that can be best developed at a university, etc.

➤ **Training Programme**: Not properly coordinated and managed.

  o **Missed Training**: Employees did not attend training.

  o **No Post Training Assessment or Coaching**: There was no assessment to verify or close skills and knowledge gaps.

3.5.4 Leadership: Motivating and Intervening

The only thing necessary for change adoption to fail is a leader or manager who does not intervene to ensure sustainable change

The leaders must support employees to adopt the change by providing the right motivation. When the change becomes normal day-to-day operations, it is extremely important that every employee's work activity is linked to an individual performance plan (IPP). The organisation and leaders need to ensure IPPs are linked to the balanced scorecard (BSC) which will measure the change programme's benefits going forward (**see Section 3.5.7**).

The leaders must also execute their third main responsibility, '**Intervene** to ensure sustainable change'. Intervention by leaders is critical to reinforce the new way of working and behaviours to ensure adoption. No matter how well the change has been implemented into the organisation, it is unlikely that every employee will adopt the change. For adoption to be successful, the leaders should be supported by the sponsor, the change team, and proactive employees at all levels of the organisation. The only things necessary for change adoption to fail are leaders and managers who do not intervene to reinforce change. Comfortable change inaction will not deliver change adoption.

Reinforcement is an effective change tool that leaders can use to encourage positive behaviours and discourage negative behaviours. It sometimes helps to provide a little motivational nudge to push employees in the right direction. The leader must also do this as part of their daily tasks. Leaders must be active and visible, intervening, communicating and reinforcing the change. There should be positive consequences for adopting the new desired behaviours, as well as negative consequences for failing to do so.

3.5.5 a2BCMF® Step 9.1 Change Adoption Assessment

Without an assessment of organisation and employee change adoption you cannot verify change implementation success

AUILM® Employee Change Adoption Assessment

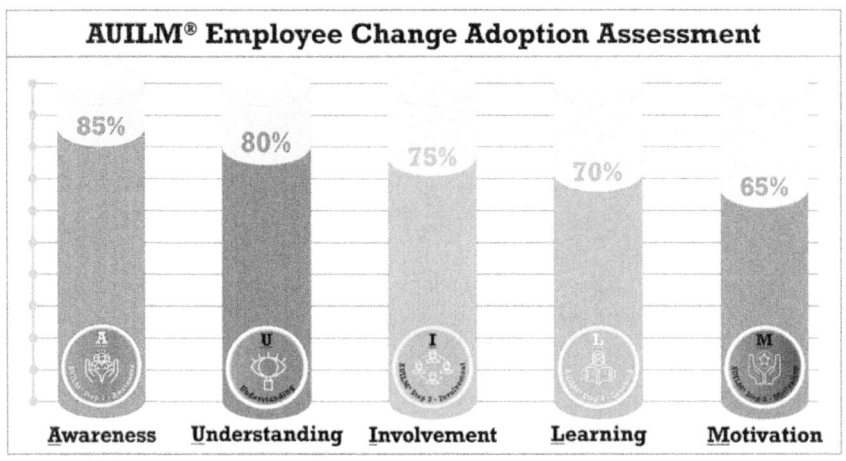

Awareness 85% | Understanding 80% | Involvement 75% | Learning 70% | Motivation 65%

Figure 3.5.5 AUILM® Change Adoption Assessment

The **AUILM®** assessment supports the wider change team to evaluate how employee change adoption is progressing as the change is being implemented. If properly executed, the assessment can identify areas within the organisation that are successfully adopting the change, as well as areas that have challenges. These challenges are opportunities for the change team to make interventions at each **AUILM®** step, implement corrective actions and get change adoption back on track. The assessment requires both quantitative and qualitative data:

- ➢ **Quantitative Data**: Designed to collect cold, hard facts, numbers, etc. Quantitative data is structured and statistical. It allows the change team to compare data and draw general conclusions from assessment data or to compare with other change programmes previously implemented in the organisation.

- ➢ **Qualitative Data**: The free text boxes collect information that seek to describe **AUILM®** employee adoption issues. They will collect employee opinions, views and reflections on change implementation progress. A qualitative survey is less structured, and it seeks to delve deeply into the assessment topics to gain information about stakeholders and employee's motivations, thinking, and attitudes.

3.5.6 a2BCMF® Step 9.2 Growth Mindset

Change leadership is about being a proactive growth mindset employee who has the knowledge, skills and ability to successfully transition an organisation from the current state 'a' to the future state 'B'

Change Management - Fixed versus Growth Mindset

Fixed Mindset
Resist disruption and change by default, it nearly always has negative impacts
- My potential is predetermined
- Setbacks are failures and the limit of our abilities
- We stick to what we know

Organisations with a growth mindset provide their employees with structural support aligning them with the organisation's processes and systems

Leaders with a growth mindset sponsor, communicate and lead the change. They are the behavioural and cultural architects

Managers with a growth mindset see the potential for employees to develop new skills and behaviours to adopt the change

Employees with a growth mindset tend to embrace and be the advocates of change, keen to adopt the new skills and behaviours

Growth Mindset
Embrace disruption and change to improve organisation
- Setbacks are opportunities to learn and develop
- Effort and attitude determine success
- We continually try new things

Enabling the Leadership of Change

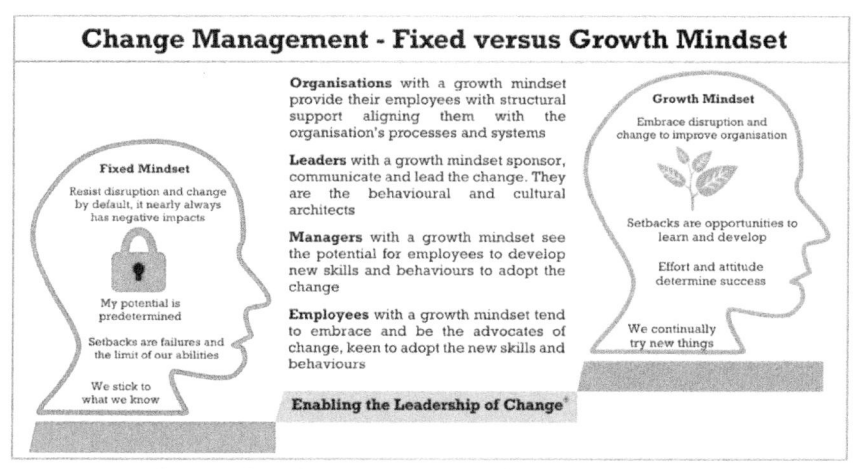

Figure 3.5.6 Fixed versus Growth Mindset

Today's organisations are in a constant state of disruption and are having to continually change, transform and innovate to keep up with changing customer buying habits and new technology. Two key challenges when implementing change are employee resistance and not learning the new skills and behaviours. These traits can be described as aspects of a *'Fixed Mindset'*, when successful change implementation really requires a *'Growth Mindset'*:

- **Fixed Mindset**: Employees with a fixed mindset think that change by default is nearly always bad and will have a negative impact on their work life.

- **Growth Mindset**: Employees with a growth mindset embrace change disruption by default, they understand the change will improve organisation performance and there will be an opportunity to develop and gain new skills.

Change teams will encounter *'Fixed Mindset'* employees and they should be aware that nothing negatively impacts organisation performance quicker than employees who resist change and who believe that the way they work today is the way they will work tomorrow.

3.5.7 a2BCMF® Step 10.1 Sustain the Change

While change programmes focus on strategy execution to improve organisation performance, shareholders at a minimum expect benefits delivery

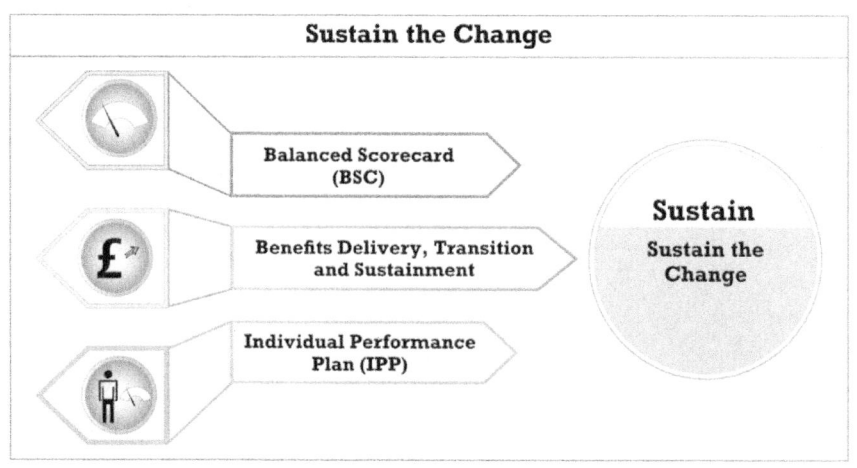

Figure 3.5.7 Sustain the Change

Sustaining the change programme is a key enabler to fulfilling the **AUILM® Motivation** step and is one of the most difficult **a2BCMF®** steps. Many organisations embark upon change programmes with the assumption that they will lead to permanent change. However, many attempts often fail to deliver sustained change or realise the intended benefits. Implementation of the following three elements can have a massive impact on sustaining the change:

> **Benefits Delivery, Transition and Sustainment**: The formally documented activities necessary to achieve the change programme's planned benefits, identifying how and when the benefits are expected to be realised.

> **Balanced Scorecard (BSC)**: An integrated set of measures built around the organisation's mission, vision and strategy, they can also be used to measure the change programme. Measures address the financial, customer, internal business processes, and learning and growth perspectives.

> **Individual Performance Plan (IPP)**: An instrument used to establish performance expectations and support the performance evaluation of each employee, usually linked to the balanced scorecard and an individual's bonus.

3.5.8 a2BCMF® Step 10.2 Close the Change Programme

The transfer of ownership from the change team to operations is often a superficial process with little or no hope of the change being sustained

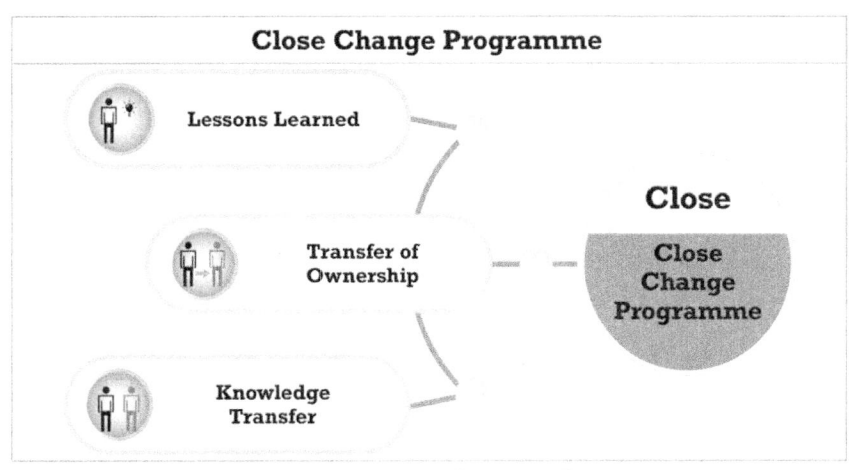

Figure 3.5.8 Close the Change Programme

The change programme closes either because its charter is fulfilled, its benefits have been fully realised, or benefits continue to be realised and managed as part of the transfer of ownership to operations. Programme governance usually approves the recommendations for the closure of the change, based on a request from the sponsor. There will be administrative activities to complete as part of formal closure, such as completing the final report. What is in included in the final report will vary for each organisation but typically it will include the following:

- **Lessons Learned**: The sum of knowledge gained from the change programme. This should be used as a reference, input and point of interest for future change programmes or projects.

- **Transfer of Ownership**: Prior to closing the change programme, the sponsor and change team should coordinate the controlled transfer of ownership to operations and receive approval to formally close out the programme.

- **Knowledge Transfer**: One of the greatest challenges at this stage of the change programme is to ensure that the experiences generated are shared with the rest of the organisation and not lost when the change team dissolves.

3.5.9 a2B Change Management Framework® Steps 9 - 10

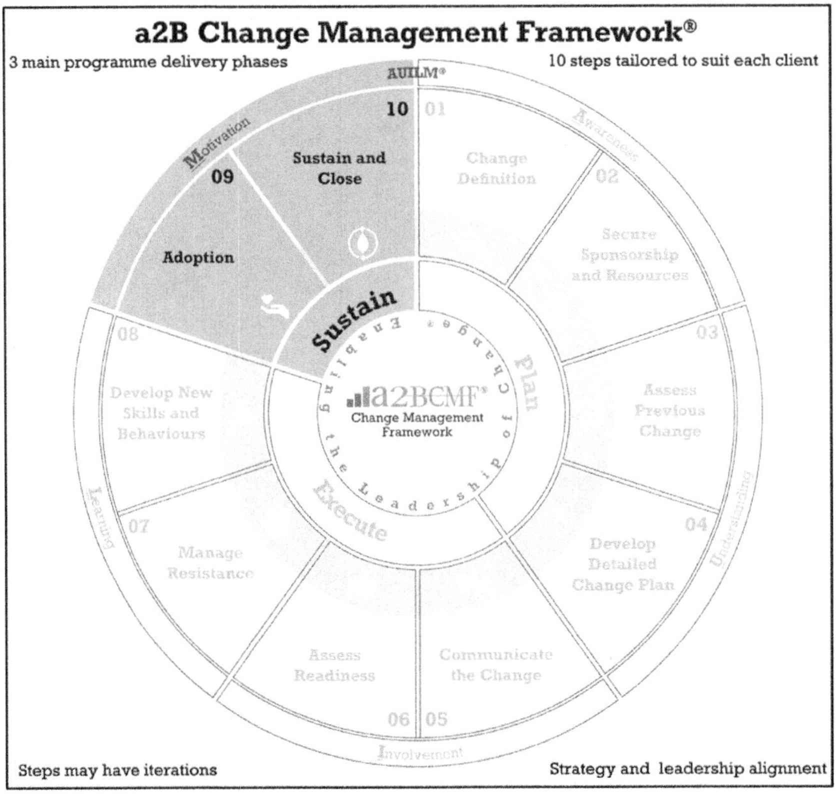

Figure 3.5.9 Change Management Framework® Steps 9 - 10

Adhering to **a2BCMF® Steps 9 and 10** can enhance employee change adoption and implementation success in the following ways:

- **Adoption**: Full adherence to the eight previous **a2BCMF®** steps ensures that the key foundations of successful change are in place. The employees must have developed the new skills and behaviours so they adopt the change to deliver improved future organisation performance.

- **Sustain and Close**: One of the most difficult tasks in change management is to sustain the change, continuing adoption and aligning new behaviours with the organisation and individual scorecards to ensure benefits realisation. The programme must have an official documented handover process to operations with tracked benefits through the BSC and IPPs. With these in place the change can then be officially closed.

Table 3.5.10 outlines some selected change concepts leaders of change should consider during the Sustain phase (**see Change Management Handbook - Leadership of Change® Volume 3**).

a2B Change Management Framework® (a2BCMF®) Considerations
Step 9 - Adoption
Change Adoption - Day One Consideration: Change adoption of the new ways of working, or system user adoption, has to be considered right at the start of the change programme or project when the change is being defined. Adoption is one of the key aims of the change, and you cannot wait until after the training to consider it.
Organisation and Employee Alignment: Achieving change adoption with a major organisational change has mixed success and the ROI benefits are not always assured. To ensure success, it is imperative that the employees are provided with new skills, behaviours and motivation so they are aligned with the: ➢ **Business Processes**: A collection of related structured activities, steps or tasks that produce a specific organisational goal. ➢ **Systems**: An organised, purposeful structure that consists of interrelated and interdependent elements. ➢ **Leadership**: A fundamental element in business success, and achieving organisation change is no different. ➢ **Communication**: One of the key levers to deliver successful change adoption. Continuous communication should motivate and align employees with the change.
Step 10 - Sustain and Close
Lessons Learned: It is important that lessons learned during the change programme are formally recorded before the change team is assigned to other programmes, new roles or leave the organisation. A key component of successful change and project management is the ability to gather key learnings from the experiences throughout the **a2BCMF®** steps.
Knowledge Transfer: One of the greatest challenges at this stage of the change programme is to ensure that the experiences generated are shared with the rest of the organisation and not lost when the change team dissolves. Knowledge transfer is a practical method of ensuring that key information is captured and stored for the future.

Table 3.5.10 Step 9 - 10 a2BCMF® Change Considerations

Section 4: Support Information

4.1 Glossary

4IR: See 'Fourth Industrial Revolution'.

5S: This approach organises the workplace, keeps it neat and clean, establishes standardised conditions and maintains discipline to sustain the effort. The name comes from the five steps required to implement the process into the workplace. The words used describe each step: **S**ort, **S**et in order, **S**hine, **S**tandardise, and **S**ustain. This is sometimes referred to as **6S** when **S**afety is included.

5 Whys: A lean technique that refers to the practice of asking, five times, why the failure has occurred in order to get to the root cause of the problem.

a2B5R® Model: Our systematic model to change employee behaviour and promote change adoption. The model has five life cycle steps: **Recognise**, **Redesign**, **Resolve**, **Replicate** and **Reinforce**.

a2B Change Management Framework®: Our **a2B Change Management Framework® (a2BCMF®)** is a structured and disciplined approach to support organisations, leadership teams and individuals going through a change, the transition from the current 'a' state to the improved future 'B' state. It has ten key steps but iterations between the steps are usually necessary and some can be worked in parallel

a2BCMF® Model: See 'a2B Change Management Framework®'.

a2BDNS© Developing the New Skills Model: Our six-step process for developing the new skills and behaviours so employees are prepared for the new way of working. The model has six process steps: **Define, Identify, Evaluate, Assess, Deliver Coach** and **Appraise**.

Actionee(s): Person(s) responsible for carrying out an action within the change programme or project.

Adoption: Change adoption is the way that the organisation and employees make the transition from the current 'a' state to the improved future 'B' state, leaving the old ways behind and adopting the new way of working and behaving. It is confirmation that they have fully accepted the change, both in mind and in heart. It is agreement that the new way of working is more efficient and benefits both the organisation and customers and is part of the organisation's future DNA.

Advocates: One of three employee change standpoints during change implementation. '**Advocates**' are similar to the change agents with their positivity towards change. Their energy should be harnessed as they can play an effective role in leading and implementing the change.

Alternative Solutions: Assessing other possible courses of action and solutions during the discussion and creation of the business case. Are there alternatives to this change programme?

Articulate: The first element of a leader's role in organisational change. Leaders are expected to **Articulate** the organisation's change vision.

AUILM® Employee Change Adoption Model: Our model outlines the five key life cycle steps the employee goes through in the change transition from the current 'a' state to the improved future 'B' state. **AUILM®** is an acronym that represents: **A**wareness, **U**nderstanding, **I**nvolvement, **L**earning and **M**otivation.

Backfire: The tendency of some leaders or employees to resist accepting evidence that conflicts with their beliefs. It causes people to strengthen their support for their original stance.

Balanced Scorecard (BSC): An integrated set of measures built around the organisation's mission, vision and strategy. Measures address the financial, customer, internal business process and learning and growth perspectives. They provide a balanced view on what is required to enact the strategy and can be used to measure the change programme.

Barrier: An impediment to successful change, these are challenges to overcome when planning, executing and sustaining change programmes. Examples might include individuals actively or passively resisting change or anything that has the potential to stop or weaken the change effort.

Baseline: The reference level against which a project, programme or portfolio is monitored and controlled.

Behaviour: The way in which employees respond to specific circumstances or situations within the workplace environment. While many elements determine an individual's behaviour in the workplace, employees are shaped by their culture and by the organisation's culture.

Behaviour Training: The training that develops the few new employee and organisation behaviours required to support change adoption. It involves defining the few critical behaviours, designing and delivering the training, and leaders modelling the new behaviours. It is supported by our **a2B5R® Model** to embed the new behaviours.

Benefit: The quantifiable and measurable improvement, resulting from completion of the change or deliverables that is perceived as positive by an organisation. It will normally have a tangible value and be expressed in monetary terms that will justify the investment. The quantitative and qualitative, measurable and non-measurable outcomes resulting from a change.

Benefits Plan and Tracker (BPT): The identification, definition, planning, tracking and realisation of business benefits as defined in the **a2BCMF® Step 1 - Change Definition**.

Benefits Realisation: The actual achievement of the change benefits which are usually delivered through the Execute and Sustain phase. This is usually the reason why most organisations undertake a change programme and is the way an organisation achieves a ROI. It will normally include a tangible value expressed in monetary terms that will justify the investment.

Budget: The sum of money allocated to the change programme. The term may also refer to revenue and expenses.

Business Case: Developed to assess the change programme's balance between costs and benefits. The business case provides business reasons for starting the change programme.

Business Operations: See 'Normal Day-to-Day Operations'.

Business Plan: A document that summarises the operational and financial objectives of an organisation and contains the detailed plans and budgets showing how the objectives are to be realised.

Business Processes: A system of activities by which a business creates a specific result for its customers. These are the foundation of how the organisation operates and, along with employees and systems, they play a significant role in organisations.

Change: The transition from the current state 'a' to the future state 'B'.

Change Agent: The individuals or groups whose task it is to effect change. They can be any member of an organisation or an external consultant involved in facilitating, supporting, influencing or implementing change. They might not be called 'change agents' as their official job title may not recognise or formalise their responsibility.

Change Blindness: A condition, where people cling onto an old belief or way of working, without considering the future or better options.

Change Capable Organisation: An organisation with developed change capability to constantly manage change successfully, maximising employee adoption and delivering sustainable benefits.

Change Capacity: The overall capacity of an organisation to either effectively prepare for, or respond to, an increasingly unpredictable planned change.

Change Communication Plan (CCP): The plan that depicts key communications, channels and the timing of these messages or events.

Change Consultant: An individual who has experience and expertise in applying change tools and techniques to resolve change problems and who can advise and facilitate an organisation's change efforts.

Change Control: Unlike the process of organisational change management, this process is about modifications to documents, deliverables, or baselines. It ensures that modifications associated with the project are identified, documented, approved, or rejected. Change control is a major aspect of the broader discipline of change management.

Change Disruption: Irreversible change that affects nearly every organisation as a result of living during the fourth industrial revolution (4IR). A period of disruption while the new change takes effect.

Change Fatigue: A general sense of apathy or passive resignation towards continual organisational changes by individuals, teams or leaders.

Change Freeze: The point at which scope changes to a programme are no longer permissible.

Change History Assessment© (CHA©): Used to assess and review the outcomes of earlier change programmes and initiatives. It provides organisational insights that may increase the likelihood of successful implementation through the analysis of lessons learned, mitigation of previous weaknesses and enhancement of future success.

Change Impact: How employees, processes, systems and the organisation are affected during the transition from the current 'a' state to the improved future 'B' state.

Change Initiative: The name given to an organisational change programme or improvement project.

Change Management: A field of management focused on organisational change which is the practice of applying a structured approach to transition an organisation from the current 'a' state to the improved future 'B' state to achieve change adoption and the expected benefits.

Change Management Framework: See 'a2B Change Management Framework'.

Change Management Gamification: An interactive and dynamic way for employees to learn change management skills and knowledge using game characteristics. Gamification can be used by employees to learn, test and prepare for organisational change.

Change Management Handbook: A book containing instructions or advice about how to do something or the most important and useful information about a subject. A reference book: in this case, practical change management implementation. This handbook contains the ten-step a2B Change Management Framework® (**a2BCMF®**) and is supported by over fifty concepts, figures, assessments, tools, templates and plans, as well as a roadmap and glossary.

Change Management Methodology: A system or approach which guides change implementation.

Change Management Pocket Guide: Typically, a small paperback that can be carried in the pocket which provides help on change management. The pocket guide contains the ten-step a2B Change Management Framework® (**a2BCMF®**) and is supported by over thirty concepts, models, figures, assessments, tools, templates, checklists and plans, as well as a roadmap and glossary.

Change Model: Models to describe and simplify a principle or define a process to develop a change deliverable.

Change Readiness Assessment (CRA): An assessment to establish if the employee and organisation are ready for change implementation. It can also gauge whether resistance will be high or low.

Change Risk: An event or condition that, if it occurs, may have an effect on change adoption and benefits realisation.

Change Saturation: When the amount of change occurring in an organisation is more than can be effectively handled by those affected by the change.

Change Sponsor Assessment (CSA): An assessment used to assess if the sponsor is performing their duties and if they are committed to the success of the change programme. The assessment should be transparent and focus on how the sponsor is performing their role with regards to **S̲ay**, **S̲upport** and **S̲ustain** activities.

Change Vision: The description of the future state 'B'. It describes how the organisation will look after the change is successfully implemented in the time limit specified.

Charter: See 'Programme Charter' and 'Project Charter'.

Checklist: A quality control technique. This may include a set of important elements that the change practitioner uses for requirement verification and validation of key change programme activities.

Coaching: A process that enables learning and development to occur and therefore performance to improve. The role of a coach is to give the employee feedback on observed performance.

Comfortable Change Inaction: The state where the immediate implication of not doing something is not visible, but in a longer run it takes a toll.

Communication Channels: The routes used to send messages, such as social media, emails, verbal presentations, reports, etc.

Competency: The organisation or individual collection of knowledge, skills, behaviours, and other characteristics and abilities to perform the role. Definitions of competencies tend to be broader than just skills.

Competency Dictionary: A tool or data structure that includes all or most of the general competencies needed to cover all job families and competencies that are core or common to all jobs within an organisation.

Competency Framework: Defines the knowledge, skills, and attributes needed for employees within an organisation. Each role will have its own set of competencies needed to perform the job effectively.

Constraint: A limitation on the change programme which could impact schedule, cost or quality of the change.

Continuous and Never-Ending Improvement (CANI): The name given to the process of always needing to improve. It is associated with growth mindset people.

Continuous Improvement (CI): The never-ending improvement of products, services or processes through incremental and breakthrough improvements. The goal is to increase effectiveness by reducing inefficiencies, frustrations, and waste (rework, time, effort, material, etc.).

Core Competence: An organisation's unique capability that would be greatly appreciated by customers and would be difficult for competitors to quickly duplicate.

Cost Overrun: This occurs when unexpected costs cause a change programme's actual cost to go beyond budget.

Critical Success Factor (CSF): A management term for an element that is necessary for an organisation or change programme to achieve its mission.

Culture: A system of shared assumptions, values and beliefs, which govern how people behave. These shared values have a strong influence on the employees in the organisation and dictate how they behave, act and perform their jobs.

Current State: The condition at the time the change is initiated, defined as the current 'a' state. The current state of the organisation's business processes, systems and employees before the change is implemented. It is often used as a baseline before the organisation moves to the future 'B' state.

Deluded Leaders: Leaders who prevent true change programme implementation because they believe (for various reasons) they are more important than the change.

Dependencies: In the project change plan, dependencies are the relationships between preceding tasks. Tasks may have multiple sub-tasks and multiple succeeding sub-tasks.

Due Diligence: One of the first steps in achieving the change programme's goals by systematically assessing the viability of the change initiative. It is effectively a risk management process designed to enable a decision on whether the change should proceed. It assesses risks, benefits, costs and impacts, providing a go/no go decision on whether the project should proceed.

Eight Wastes of Lean: TIM H WOOD is an acronym for the 8 wastes commonly found within business: Transport, Inventory, Motion, Human, Waiting, Over production, Over processing and Defects.

Emotional Intelligence: The ability to monitor your emotions or the emotions of others and use this to guide your actions during the change. Leaders of change need to recognise and regulate emotions in themselves and others. As change management professionals, we engage employees and impacted stakeholders, relying on them to adopt the change and ensure benefits realisation.

Employee: An individual who was hired by an employer to perform a specific role that adds value to the organisation. Successful change depends on **AUILM®** and/or **a2B5R®** support. Along with processes and systems, they play a significant role in organisations.

Employee Behaviour: The way in which employees respond to specific circumstances or changes in the workplace.

Employee Engagement: A workplace approach resulting in the right conditions for all employees of an organisation to feel passionate about their jobs, be committed to their organisation's goals and values, and be motivated to contribute to organisational change and success.

Employee Process System Data (EPSD): Four critical elements that need to be aligned by the change team during organisational change implementation.

Employees, Processes, Systems and Leaders (EPSL): Four critical elements that the organisation needs to align to deliver successful change.

Enabler: A positive facilitator to successful change. These can be individuals actively or passively supporting change or anything that has the potential to improve change implementation success.

Entitlement: Employees with a sense of entitlement believe that they are owed favours by the organisation and should get what they want because of who they are. Others might observe their worthiness as unrealistic, unmerited, or inappropriate.

Estimated Completion Date (ECD): The expected date an action or deliverable should be complete.

Execute Phase: The second phase of the a2B Change Management Framework® (steps five to eight) which focus on change implementation.

Facilitator: The person responsible for guiding and supporting employees through the change process interactively.

Fixed Mindset: Employees with a fixed mindset will, by default, reject and resist disruption and change. This will prevent true change. Their assumption is that change is usually always bad, and they stick what they know.

Fourth Industrial Revolution (4IR): Describes exponential change in the way we live, work and relate to one another. 4IR includes the adoption of cyber-physical systems, the Internet of Things and the Internet of Systems.

Frame of Reference: A set of criteria or stated values in relation to perceptions and judgements that can be made by employees. How the employee or change target interprets what they see in terms of their own cultural frame of reference.

Future State: The future state 'B', when employees have adopted the new way of working and the benefits have been realised.

Governance: The decision-making processes, applied by authorised individuals or teams, for approving/rejecting, monitoring and adjusting activities of the project change plan (PCP).

Growth Mindset: These employees embrace disruption and change to improve organisation performance. Setbacks are opportunities to learn (CANI) and an individual's effort and attitude determine success.

Hubris: Leaders with excessive pride and over confidence which manifests itself as a major barrier to change implementation success.

Hunch and Launch Syndrome: A name given to the process of coming up with a change idea (hunch) and then introducing (launch) it into the organisation without strategic consideration or a plan on how the benefits will be realised. These ideas rarely deliver strategic change or sustainable benefits and are sometimes referred to as 'pet projects'.

Individual Performance Plan (IPP): An instrument used to establish performance expectations and to support the performance evaluation of each employee, usually linked to the balanced scorecard and an individual's bonus.

Intervene: The third element of a leader's role in organisational change. They should **Intervene** when they observe an employee resisting change, or when employees are not adopting the new skills and behaviours.

Intervention: All the planned programme activities that aim to bring changes into an organisation. They are led by the sponsor and the leadership team.

Key Performance Indicators (KPI): A set of quantifiable measures that a company uses to gauge its performance over time. These metrics are used to determine an organisation's progress in achieving its strategic (change) and operational goals. They also compare a company's finances and performance against other businesses within its industry.

Knowledge Transfer: The process of transferring knowledge from the change programme to other parts or systems within the organisation. Like knowledge management, knowledge transfer seeks to capture, organise, create, or distribute knowledge and ensure its availability for future change teams.

Leader: A person in the organisation who is responsible for leading; directing, commanding, or guiding a group or activity. Without a leader leading the change programme it is likely to fail. The leader's role in organisational change is to **Articulate** the change vision, **Model** the new behaviours and **Intervene** to reinforce the change.

Leadership: The leaders of the organisation who are collectively responsible for strategy execution and its inherent change programmes.

Leadership Alignment: This process develops change leadership capability, so the organisation's leaders are aligned, as a high performing team, with change leadership skills and knowledge to successfully lead the organisation's change,

transformation or improvement to accelerate employee change adoption and deliver sustainable long-term benefits.
Leadership of Change®: The ability to lead, support, influence and enthuse those involved in organisation change to transition from the current 'a' state to the improved future 'B' state to achieve change adoption and the expected benefits.
Lean: A process improvement methodology, focused on reducing waste in a system. The term lean is derived from the idea that the approach reduces 'waste' that contributes to inefficient processes and poor outcomes.
Lessons Learned: The sum of knowledge gained from the change programme. This should be used as a reference, input and point of interest for future change programmes or projects.
Master Project Plan: The wider project plan that drives the change or transformation across the organisation and coordinates activities performed by the work streams. The project change plan (PCP) should be aligned with the key milestones on the master project plan and both plans should be updated simultaneously. In some cases, there may only be a single PCP.
Mentoring: A process of providing support, challenge and extension of the learning of one person through the guidance of another who is more knowledgeable and experienced.
Merger: The combination of two or more separate companies into one. Most mergers involve the integration of operations, processes, assets, management and organisations.
Milestone: An important date or deadline, the start or end of significant phases of work shown on the project change plan (PCP). It is usually reflected as a diamond symbol.
Mission: Describes the overall purpose of the organisation. Each organisation's statement can vary widely in terms of content, stretch and scope.
Model: The second element of a leader's role in organisational change. It is an activity expected from the organisation's leader (and sponsor). They should **Model** the new skills and behaviours, providing a role model to other staff.
Narcissistic Leader: A leader with excessive self-confidence and an obsessive focus on their personal image, accompanied by contempt for anyone who thinks that the organisation's strategic change programme is more important than them.
Normal Day-to-Day Operations: The activities that an organisation and its employees engage in on a daily basis for the purposes of generating a profit and increasing the inherent value of the organisation.
Observers: One of three employee change standpoints during change implementation. '**Observers**' will monitor the '**Advocates**' and assess if the change is benefiting them. If this appears positive, they will tend to move towards being receptive to the change.
Organisation: A social arrangement for achieving controlled performance in pursuit of collective goals.
Organisational Agility: The ability of an organisation to respond to ambiguity, threats, opportunities or uncertainty with flexibility and speed.

Organisational Development (OD): A process for instigating, implementing and sustaining change, it involves activities that impact employees, the team and the organisation.

Outcome: A specific measurable result or effect of an action or situation.

Pet Projects: Projects directed or supported by the CEO or other senior leaders that appeal to their emotions and hubris, they rarely deliver strategic value.

Plan Phase: The first phase of the a2B Change Management Framework® (steps one to four) which focus on change planning.

Planned Change: An intentional intervention for bringing about change to an organisation. It is best characterised as deliberate, purposeful and systematic.

Process: See business process.

Programme: A group of related projects, sub-programmes and programme activities that are managed in a coordinated way to obtain benefits not available by managing them individually. (**a2BCMF®** uses this default name for change initiatives, each client organisation can refer to them as programmes, projects, etc.)

Programme Charter: A document that details the scope, organisation, and objectives of a programme. It authorises the programme sponsor or manager to use the organisational resources to deliver the programme. The programme charter may include various project charters.

Project: A temporary endeavour undertaken to create a unique product, service, change or result.

Project Change Plan (PCP): The plan to deliver the change programme. (The words project and programme can be interchangeable depending on the makeup of the change initiative, it can be either a project or programme).

Project Charter: A document that details the scope, organisation, and objectives of a project. It authorises the project sponsor or manager to use the organisational resources to deliver the project.

Project Management: The application of knowledge, skills, tools, and techniques to achieve project activities to meet the project requirements.

Project Management Office (PMO): An organisational unit that oversees project (change) management related activities within an organisation. It seeks to facilitate and expedite project and change work through the use of standard procedures.

Qualitative Data: Information that seeks to describe a topic more than measure it, such as opinions, views and reflections. A qualitative survey is less structured, and it seeks to delve deeply into the assessment topics to gain information about stakeholders and employee's motivations, thinking, and attitudes.

Quantitative Data: Cold, hard facts and numbers. Quantitative data is structured and statistical. It provides support when you need to draw general conclusions from your assessment or research.

Rarely Blame the Employee (RBtE): Employees should rarely be blamed, as we don't know their environment or background. Only the behaviours they are exhibiting should be judged.

Readiness: The process of assessing the change readiness of the organisation and the employees prior to change implementation. This will ensure change can be adopted and the benefits can be realised.

REBELs: One of three employee change standpoints during change implementation. '**REBELs**' tend to resist change blindly, sometimes this can be a natural reaction even if the change is to their benefit. The default reaction is that change is a bad thing and will put them at a disadvantage.

Reinforce: Reinforcing change is critical to ensure adoption of the new way of working. The sponsor and leaders are expected to intervene when there is resistance, or when the employees are not adopting the new skills and behaviours.

Resistance: The reaction by the organisation, departments or individuals when they perceive that an organisational change coming their way could be a threat to them. Without further awareness and understanding, this resistance will cause fear. It will trigger actions that negatively impact the pace of organisational change implementation, adoption of the new ways of working and benefits delivery.

Resistance Management: The process of addressing stakeholders' opposition to a change.

Resistance Strategy Plan (RSP): This plan provides specific actions to understand and address resistance. The actions and plan focus on the change implementation strategy and vary depending on if it is a '**Tell**' or '**Sell**' change implementation approach. This is a component plan of the PCP and may be needed if the change team foresees high resistance challenges.

Return on Investment (ROI): The benefits that the change delivers. These are dependent on speed of adoption as well as delivering the programme on time, within budget and the specified scope. The ROI can be calculated using the following equation, ROI = (Expected Project Benefits - Project Costs) / Project Costs.

Rework: Correcting a defective, failed, or non-conforming item, service or product prior to customer delivery. Rework includes an organisation's repeat effort, such as disassembly, repair, replacement, reassembly, etc.

Risk: See 'Change Risk'.

Roadmap: A chronological representation of a programme's intended direction, graphically depicting dependencies between major milestones and decision points, while communicating the linkage between the organisation's strategy and the programme's work.

Say: The first key element of sponsorship. **Say** is the foundation and is all about communicating the business case for the change to all affected stakeholders.

Servant Leadership: A leadership philosophy in which the main goal of the leader is to serve others, focussing on the needs of employees, especially team members, before they consider themselves. Leaders do not accrue power or take control. The characteristics of servant leadership are compulsory to be an effective and proactive leader of change.

Skills: Transferable talent, competence, expertise, etc needed by the employee to be able to operate at the new way of working. These will include technical understanding and subject knowledge.

Skills and Behaviours Learning Plan: Identifies skills and behaviours that will be required for the employees to adapt to the new way of working. A training needs analysis (TNA) can be used to identify skill and behaviour gaps. This is a component plan of the PCP and may be needed if the change team foresees learning or training as a major activity in terms of effort and time.

SIPOC: A process improvement tool used for documenting business processes. SIPOC stands for Suppliers, Inputs, Process, Outputs, and Customers which often form the columns of the diagram. The SIPOC diagram visually illustrates a business process from beginning to end at a high level.

Sponsor: The most senior leader within the programme, reporting to the CEO or a steering committee. They are authorised to mandate the programme, the business case and are responsible for change adoption, benefits realisation and successful change programme delivery.

Sponsorship: The sponsorship role is to communicate the programme's change (**Say**), provide resources (**Support**) and ensure the change lasts (**Sustain**), the process of aligning stakeholders to support and own the change.

Sponsorship and Resource Plan: Identifies the change sponsor and defines the strategy and actions to develop the required programme resources; change lead, communication lead, change agents, etc. This is a component plan of the PCP and may be needed if the change team foresees resourcing their team as a challenge.

Sponsor Assessment: An assessment of the organisation's sponsorship that can identify strengths or weaknesses with the change implementation.

Stakeholder: An individual affected or impacted by a change.

Stakeholder Analysis: The systematic examination and evaluation of stakeholders in order to prioritise, manage and engage with them effectively throughout the change programme.

Stakeholder Engagement: The process in which an organisation involves and engages people who may be affected by the decisions it makes or can influence the implementation of the change.

Stakeholder Engagement Plan: Identifies the actions to engage groups and individuals affected by the change and mitigate resistance by enlisting their support, adoption and ownership. This is a component plan of the PCP and may be needed if the change team foresees stakeholder engagement challenges.

Stakeholder Mapping: This involves representing stakeholders on a grid to display their level of influence on one axis from low to high, and their likely level of cooperation '**REBELs**', '**Observers**' and '**Advocates**' toward the change on the other.

Standard Operating Procedure (SOP): Top-level documents that advise employees which actions to take under a variety of circumstances. Standard work instructions (SWI) describe those actions in detail.

Standard Work Instructions (SWI): Lower-level detailed instructions designed to ensure that an organisation's manufacturing and service processes are consistent, timely and repeatable. Leading practice suggests SWI are printed and located near the operator's workstation.

Strategic Planning: The process undertaken by an organisation to define its overall purpose, priorities to work towards that purpose and how each priority will be addressed.

Strategy: An approach to achieve an organisation's strategic goals or address strategic issues. A strategy might be a major approach that uses the internal strengths of an organisation to take advantage of external opportunities, while shoring up internal weaknesses to ward off external threats. An organisation's strategies are usually long-term.

Subject Matter Expert (SME): An individual who exhibits the highest level of expertise in performing a specialised job, task, or skill within the organisation and can be an invaluable resource to the change team.

Support: The second key element of sponsorship. **Support** builds on **Say** and in this element the sponsor starts to actively and overtly support the change, provide resources and coach the organisation.

Sustain: The third key element of sponsorship. It builds on **Say** and **Support**. **Sustain** is critical for the organisation to deliver value and achieve its strategic goals.

Sustain and Close Plan: The sustain part of the plan provides an approach to sustaining adoption and benefits realisation. The close plan will officially transfer ownership and close off the programme, ensuring administrative activities are completed as per the organisation's procedures. This is a component plan of the PCP and may be needed if the change team foresees sustaining and closing the change as challenging.

Sustain Phase: The third phase of the **a2B Change Management Framework®** (steps nine and ten) which focus on closing the change programme to sustain adoption and ensure benefits realisation.

Sustainability: The ability to maintain the future state 'B'.

System: A set of interconnected devices that provide outputs. They execute and control the internal processes and procedures that deliver the organisation's products or services. Along with employees and processes, they play a significant role in organisations.

System Change: An organisational change that focuses on changing its internal systems which manage and control the internal processes and procedures that deliver its products or services.

System Operating Manual (SOM): The documentation by which an organisation provides guidance on how employees should operate the referenced business system. It documents the approved standard procedures for performing steps correctly and reasonably efficiently to produce goods and provide services.

Tactic: A series of activities, usually short-term and small in scale, intended to achieve a goal or objective.

Threat: A negative risk that could adversely affect the change programme's objectives.

To-Be State: See 'Future State'.

Training Needs Analysis (TNA): The process in which the organisation identifies the training and development needs of its employees so that they can do their job effectively.

Training Plan: A detailed plan for how the organisation, groups and individuals will be trained and coached so they have the new skills and behaviours to perform the new way of working. It will include the training objectives, how and who will develop the content, the selection process of who will be trained, when they will be trained, who will deliver the training, how the trainers will be trained, assessment criteria and coaching plans.

Transfer of Ownership: Prior to closing the change programme, the sponsor and change team should coordinate the controlled transfer of ownership to operations and receive approval to formally close out the programme.

Transformation: Fundamental changes that are significant and considered vital to the future success of the organisation.

Transition State: The state between the current 'a' and future 'B' state. Transition state is the process of equipping the employees with skills and behaviours to adopt the new way of working so the organisation can achieve benefits realisation.

Triple Constraint: The combination of the three most significant restrictions on any change programme or project; scope, schedule and cost.

Values Statement: Describes the overall, top-level priorities for how an organisation chooses to conduct its activities and to be viewed by the public, for example, integrity, efficiency and reliability.

Vision: See 'Change Vision'.

Vision Statement: A vivid and compelling description of the organisation and its customers at some time in the future. It depicts a long-term, inspirational and strategic vision, which describes the organisation and customers shortly after the strategic plan has been implemented.

WIIFM (What's In It For Me): This concept focuses on the likelihood of employee acceptance. The basic premise of this acronym is that when the result of an action is in the best interests of an employee, they are more likely to choose to do it.

Work Stream: A team or group of individuals who complete a common set of activities or tasks as part of a bigger change programme.

Yes Men and Women: Employees who agree with deluded leaders when they know that this will damage or delay change implementation.

4.2 Afterword

Organisation change implementation is unlikely to be successful without maximising employee change adoption. Employees and shareholders of organisations are now starting to demand that organisations have **Leadership of Change**® capability in their change practitioners, leaders, sponsors and those directly supporting organisation change. Change professionals, leaders, sponsors and the change team should support employees through the change transition, enhancing it so it is a positive experience. Treat the employees well so they feel valued, motivated, committed to their organisation's goals and values and contribute to organisational change success. With full adoption, the organisation can achieve sustainable change and benefits realisation.

I hope this book has enabled you to gain insights into change management adoption and help you on your **Leadership of Change**® journey. It should help you to understand and support employees through the change transition by providing **A**wareness, **U**nderstanding, **I**nvolvement, **L**earning, and **M**otivation (**AUILM**®) for the change.

Thank you for purchasing and reading this book. If you have enjoyed reading it, please submit an honest review to your local Amazon website so that others may assess its value to their own change management and leadership learning journey.

If you wish to find out more about the **Leadership of Change**®, please visit:

www.peterfgallagher.com/leadership-of-change

If your organisation would like to learn more about our consultancy services, please visit:

www.a2B.consulting

Or contact me directly by email:

peter.gallagher@a2B.consulting

4.3 About the Author

Peter is a Change Management Expert, International Speaker, Author, Leadership Alignment Coach and Trusted Adviser to C-suites.

He has a proven track record of complex change and project delivery in multi-disciplinary environments for the world's largest and most successful organisations. He has Big Four external consulting experience, as well as internal and commercial consulting experience, working in over thirty countries over a thirty-year career. Companies he has worked for include: EY, Shell, NCR and Bombardier Aerospace. Peter has also held senior roles in industry and has boardroom experience as a NED. His clients include organisations such as ADNOC, Boeing, BP, GE, Rolls Royce and Aramco.

Peter speaks on the **Leadership of Change**®, change management, change leadership alignment and the benefits of change management gamification. As a speaker, Peter has presented strategic transformations leading practice to Government entities, CEO audiences globally, leadership teams and at professional membership conferences. For over thirty years, Peter has been helping organisations, leaders and employees change, improve and transform through keynotes, masterclasses, change management gamification workshops, projects and programmes. The change question set Peter asks all leaders is:

"Do you understand your organisation's change history? Do you have a change vision? Are you aligned on your strategic objectives? Are you a high performing team? Does your team have change leadership skills to lead the change or improvement that your organisation is facing?"

He then works with their leadership team to develop the solution.

Peter has an MBA (Distinction) from the Robert Gordon University. He is an American Society of Quality (ASQ) Certified Manager of Quality, a Certified Change Management Professional™ with the Association of Change Management Professionals® (ACMP®) and holds three certifications from the Project Management Institute (PMI). He is also a Lean Six Sigma Master Black Belt. He is a member of the global board of directors for the Association of Change Management Professionals® (ACMP®).

4.4 Other Leadership of Change® Volumes
Change Management Body of Knowledge (CMBoK)

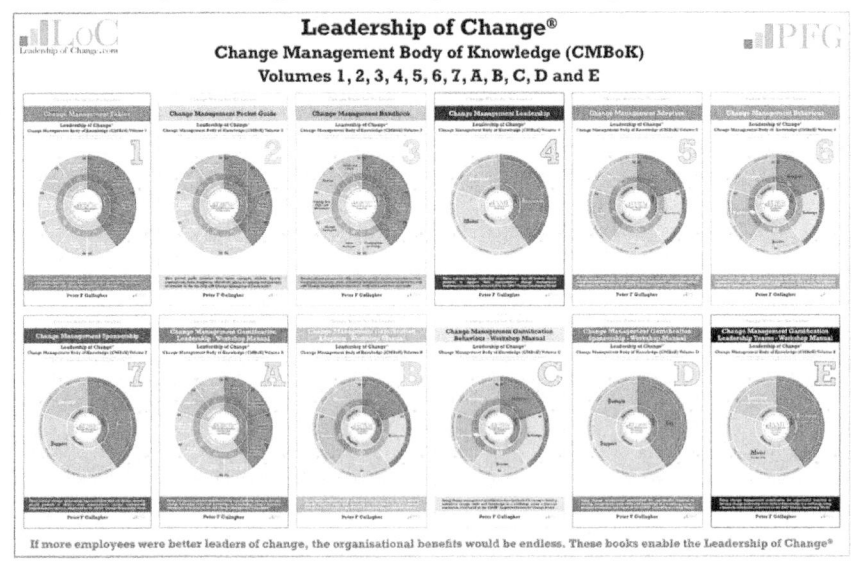

Change Management Fables - Leadership of Change® Volume 1
Ten fables about the leadership paradox of implementing organisational change management versus delivering normal day-to-day operations, structured on the **a2B Change Management Framework®**.

Change Management Pocket Guide - Leadership of Change® Volume 2
This pocket guide contains over thirty concepts, models, figures, assessments, tools, templates, checklists, plans, a roadmap and glossary, structured on the ten-step **a2B Change Management Framework®**.

Change Management Handbook - Leadership of Change® Volume 3
This handbook contains over fifty concepts, models, figures, assessments, tools, templates, checklists, plans, a roadmap and glossary, structured on the ten step **a2B Change Management Framework®** each with a practical case study.

Change Management Leadership - Leadership of Change® Volume 4
Effective and proactive leadership is essential for successful organisational change. This book outlines the three critical leadership responsibilities to implement change: **Articulate** the vision, **Model** the new way and **Intervene** to ensure sustainable change, structured on the **AMI® Change Leadership Model**.

Change Management Adoption - Leadership of Change® Volume 5
Achieving employee change adoption in a major organisation change or transformation has mixed success, and the ROI benefits are not always realised. For change adoption to be successful, the leaders, sponsor and change team should support employees through the change transition by providing **Awareness**, **Understanding**, **Involvement**, **Learning**, and **Motivation** for the change, structured on the **AUILM® Employee Change Adoption Model**.

4.4 Other Leadership of Change® Volumes

Change Management Behaviour - Leadership of Change® Volume 6
Behaviour change is sometimes required in order for an organisation to successfully deliver change or transformations to achieve sustainable change and benefits realisation. To change these behaviours, the organisation must support employees through the change transition by implementing five key change behaviour life cycle steps: **Recognise**, **Redesign**, **Resolve**, **Replicate** and **Reinforce**, structured on the **a2B5R® Employee Behaviour Change Model**.

Change Management Sponsorship - Leadership of Change® Volume 7
Without an effective and proactive change sponsor, most change programmes or initiatives will fail to achieve the targeted objectives. This book outlines the three critical sponsorship responsibilities to successfully implement change: **Say**, **Support**, and **Sustain** structured on the **a2B3S® Change Sponsorship Model**.

Change Management Gamification Leadership - Leadership of Change® Volume A
This change management gamification workshop manual supports organisational leaders to learn about change leadership in a workshop environment using a business simulation. It includes a business case study that enables experiential learning in a safe environment so the skills and knowledge can be immediately applied back in the workplace.

Change Management Gamification Adoption - Leadership of Change® Volume B
This change management gamification workshop manual supports change professionals to learn about change implementation with a focus on employee change adoption in a workshop environment using a business simulation. It includes a business case study that enables experiential learning in a safe environment so the skills and knowledge can be immediately applied back in the workplace.

Change Management Gamification Behaviour - Leadership of Change® Volume C
This change management gamification workshop manual supports change professionals to learn about change implementation with a focus on changing employee behaviours in a workshop environment using a business simulation. It includes a business case study that enables experiential learning in a safe environment so the skills and knowledge can be immediately applied back in the workplace.

Change Management Gamification Sponsorship - Leadership of Change® Volume D
This change management gamification workshop manual supports change sponsors to learn about change implementation with a focus on their three main change sponsorship responsibilities in a workshop environment using a business simulation. It includes a business case study that enables experiential learning in a safe environment so the skills and knowledge can be immediately applied back in the workplace.

Change Management Gamification Leadership Teams - Leadership of Change® Volume E
This change management gamification workshop manual supports leadership teams to learn about change implementation with a focus on their three main change management leadership responsibilities in a workshop environment using a business simulation. It includes a business case study that enables experiential learning in a safe environment so the skills and knowledge can be immediately applied back in the workplace.

4.5 Connect with Me Online

Connect with me online to learn more about our latest products and services, read our blog, and learn more about how to join the conversation about change management!

We would love to hear your story. If you try something and it works, let us know! Equally, if you tried something and it failed, we would like to hear from you!

www.peterfgallagher.com/leadership-of-change

Join the conversation

Linked in peterfgallagher

@peterfgallagher

Please contact **Peter** through his website at:
www.peterfgallagher.com

For **Consultancy Services** please contact us through our website at:
www.a2B.consulting